HEALING THE ONE NEW MAN

HEALING THE ONE NEW MAN

Restoring the Church's Identity Through the Feasts

MATTHEW MOORE

HTONM

Contents

Dedication — ix

Acknowledgements — xi

Introduction — xiii

1 Addressing Antisemitism — 1

2 A Revelation — 11

3 What Next? — 21

4 The One New Man — 27

5 God's Design for the Church — 33

6 Breaking the Church's Identity — 43

7 Healing and Core Identity — 55

8 Restoring the Church's Identity — 61

9 Uprooting False Beliefs — 67

10 The Lord's Festivals and the Church's Identity — 71

11 "God's Appointed Times" Not "The Jewish Feasts" — 81

12 The Feasts of the Lord and God as Creator — 89

13 Messiah in the Feasts - Sabbath — 93

14 Messiah in the Feasts - Passover — 107

15 Messiah in the Feasts – Firstfruits   113

16 Messiah in the Feasts - Pentecost   117

17 Messiah in the Feasts - Trumpets   125

18 Messiah in the Feasts – The Day of Atonement   129

19 Messiah in the Feasts – Tabernacles   135

20 Challenges to Healing the One New Man   143

21 They're All About Worship   153

22 The Feasts as a Prophetic Timeline   159

23 Put Yourself in the Sheet   167

Appendix 1   177
Appendix 2   181
Appendix 3   185
End Notes   187

Dedication

To the three ladies that bring me the most joy in my life: my wife Becky and my two daughters, Regan and Riley. Thank you.

Acknowledgements

I am grateful for my parents and other spiritual leaders from my childhood who planted the seeds of a Biblical understanding of God's heart for the nation and people of Israel.

My parents raised me in a godly home. They established in me a firm foundation in Scripture, the importance of a devotional life, and, by example, a life dedicated to obeying God and walking by faith.

My wife, Becky, and my daughters, Regan and Riley, bring me great joy as they live out their God-given identities, becoming who God made them to be. They are a constant source of encouragement to me in my own walk of faith.

I'm also grateful for the many brothers and sisters I have served alongside in Ellel Ministries over the past decade. They have been instrumental in bringing light, truth, and restoration into my life. It has been through their sacrificial service and godly influence that I have been healed and delivered so that I could share with others what the Lord has revealed to me and I have related in this book.

Finally, I want to thank all those who have prayed for me so faithfully. There are many intercessors the Lord has sent my way. In addition to my parents, several individuals have been steadfast intercessors including Anita Lynott, Lori Chirico, Kathie Taflinger, Mary Whitmire, Pinky (Maria) Mejia, the Ellel USA ministry team, and my dear Ugandan friend, Pastor Geoffrey Baluwine and his church, to name just a few. Only God knows how much their prayers have impacted my life.

Above all, I acknowledge the Lord Jesus, who through His Holy Spirit has delivered me, renewed and transformed my mind, and helped me to pursue the fullness of His purposes in my life.

Introduction

I have consistently observed, over my many years as a Christian, that where division and disunity reign among a group of believers (whether it be in a church or parachurch organization), the movement of the Holy Spirit is quenched. This is particularly true in relation to the work of the Holy Spirit in bringing physical, emotional, or spiritual healing. By contrast, where spiritual unity among diverse cultures and backgrounds is brought about through Christian unity, the presence and power of the Holy Spirit seems to flow freely. Healing is a gift and a blessing. The Lord spoke through David in Psalm 133 affirming the power of unity and promising to command a blessing when God's people dwell in unity.

Which comes first, unity or the free flow of the Holy Spirit? The intersection of these two concepts is a mystery, much like the sovereignty of God and the free will of man. What seems certain, however, is that unity and the presence and power of the Holy Spirit are closely related. Where one exists, the Other will be manifest. Thus, where disunity exists among believers, we can assume that the Holy Spirit's work is being hindered. Similarly, if the Holy Spirit is not moving, we must consider whether ungodly disunity exists.

This does not mean that we seek "unity at all costs." Paul admonishes us not to be yoked with unbelievers. We should not seek peace and unity with the world, the flesh, or the devil. In fact, the Scriptures clearly teach we should separate ourselves from the world and worldly behaviors.

But, among believers, it must be possible to enjoy a godly form of unity that respects individuality and the uniqueness of each person's giftings and identity while at the same time being unified in a way that the Holy Spirit's presence and power can manifest through us so the kingdom of darkness is daily being assailed.

This is the premise of "Healing the One New Man". It seems obvious that we are not experiencing the power and presence of the Holy Spirit to the degree Jesus said we should and would. In fact, the current church is not even manifesting the work of the Holy Spirit in the same way as the Church in the book of Acts. Similarly, no one can seriously argue that there is unity within the Church. Hundreds of denominations now exist, and they continue to multiply exponentially. Why?

Over the centuries, many books and much thought and discussion have been dedicated to the issue of disunity in the church. Paul's seemingly idyllic description of what he calls the "one new man" in the second chapter of his epistle to the Ephesians certainly doesn't exist in the Church today.

A resurgence of interest in unity arose in the early 1900s with the birth of what some call the ecumenical movement. From this movement arose a movement toward non-denominationalism. Non-denominational churches represent some of the fastest growing churches in the world today. Nevertheless, the number of denominations since 1900 has increased 3000%.

In discussing the One New Man in this book, I assume a commonality in core evangelical Christian theological beliefs including: the Trinity, the virgin birth, salvation by grace through faith alone in the finished work of Jesus upon the cross, His physical resurrection from the dead, and His literal return to this earth to rule and reign as King, and a personal relationship with God manifest through the indwelling work of the Holy Spirit. I also consider the Bible to be the inspired Word of God in the original autographs, and should be used to inform and test all spiritual teaching. I am not endorsing the so-called interfaith movement that seeks "unity" among all religions. Jesus is the only way of salvation. He is the Truth and the Life and the only Way to be reconciled with God the Father.

Having clarified the group I am defining as the One New Man, it is painfully obvious that among the group I've described, we have not achieved anything close to what Jesus pled for in John 17. In fact, the more time that passes since Jesus walked the earth in the flesh, the more disunified we seem to become, with the number of denominations and distinct religious organizations exponentially increasing since the time of the birth of the ecumenical movement until today.

This begs the question: Why, with so much effort and thought on the matter, and certainly a desire among many to see a more unified front against our common enemy (satan) and the spiritual darkness that seems to now be enveloping the earth, are we seemingly unable to tear down walls of division within the Body of Christ?

A major root to disunity lies hidden in the history of the church – all the way back to the second, third and fourth centuries after Christ's ascension. Uprooting this false teaching is a key to releasing the Church into the unity Paul describes in Ephesians 2.

As Jesus well noted, a good tree cannot bear bad fruit nor can a bad tree bear good fruit, but each tree bears fruit after its own kind. This is certainly true regarding the source of division in the church.

A good definition of healing that we often use in Ellel Ministries when teaching on the topic is: "restoring God's order." Our experience is, when we help people bring their lives into godly order by addressing areas where God's ways have either not been known or followed, and lead them to recognize and apply simple Kingdom principles Jesus taught related to those areas, healing is a natural response. We've literally seen thousands of people over the course of three decades, from hundreds of different cultural, ethnic, and religious backgrounds, experience physical, emotional, and spiritual healing when we apply these principles.

One of the most important parts of beginning the healing process is asking the Lord to reveal the root of the problem. Through my involvement in the healing ministry, I have come to learn that we are in an uphill battle to help bring wholeness in an individual's life if they are unwilling to dig down to the places where the wounds and brokenness are hidden and where the bad fruit that is manifesting in their lives is rooted. This requires recognizing and admitting the wounding and related pain that started the growth of the bad roots which are producing the bad fruit, and dealing with those roots by confessing sinful responses to the wounding, forgiving others and self, expressing consequent emotions in a godly way and experiencing the Lord's touch in the place of the wounding.

This process often also requires replacing false beliefs, which are a frequent byproduct of these experiences, with God's truth. Renunciation of words and behaviors that have grown out of those false beliefs are also key to the healing process. But it all starts with identifying the root.

These wounds, and consequent beliefs, behave much like a strangler fig, especially when the beliefs are affecting the core identity of an individual. The strangler fig is an invasive species that attaches to a normal tree in subtropical forests. It is a form of banyan tree. Florida has many trees affected by strangler figs. They typically start out with a pod nestling itself into the crook of a branch of the host tree's trunk. The strangler fig then grows, putting out vines that begin to hang down from the branches where the pod is lodged and connect to the ground or wrap around the trunk of the tree.

Over time, the host tree becomes covered with these vines that begin to appear as if they are part of the tree, when, in fact, they are killing the host tree. If left unchecked, they will destroy the original tree, replacing it with a shell of banyan vines that have solidified into what looks like a tree trunk. Often, the hollow center where the original tree once thrived can be seen. The host tree is dead.

By analogy, ungodly false beliefs that become rooted in a person's identity can do the same thing to their victim. When an ungodly belief is adopted and incorporated into our life and acted upon consistently over time, it will ultimately "strangle" our God-given identity and push forward a false identity that bears little resemblance to God's original design for us.

In the same manner, to bring healing to the bad fruit of division and fracture in the Body of Christ, we must dig up the roots for these and deal with them just as we would with a personal wound and consequent false beliefs. We need to ask the Lord to show us the things that are and are not part of the Church's God-given identity. What beliefs are part of the "strangler fig's" operation to destroy the Church? I pray that this book will help the Church consider the broken places in its past and allow the Lord to heal the wounding that served to start and feed the division that now exists in the Church. In short, my hope is that this book will provide a guide to restoring God's order to His Body and thereby restore the Church's true identity.

The fruit of many healing needs within an individual relates back to disunity or dissonance in the individual's root identity. Similarly, the root of the problem of disunity in the Church and the consequential "bad fruit" lies in the confounding of the Church's core identity as grafted into God's Covenant relationship with Israel. The "root of the root" of the Church's identity is, of course, Jesus. But the cultivated "Olive Tree" in the Apostle Paul's analogy in Romans Chapter 11 was the nation and people of Israel and the covenantal relationship God formed with them.

As believers in Jesus, born-again Christians should identify in those Covenants, and the benefits of them should be enjoyed by such believers even though they are not of the physical blood line of those with whom the Covenant was made. This is the miracle of Jesus' work on the Cross that grafts us Gentiles into these promises of the Old Covenant by our simple faith in Him.

But note that to lay claim to the promises of the Old Covenant, the Church must identify with it. Rejection of the Old Covenant – treating it as if it has nothing to do with the "modern" born-again believer – is akin to rejecting our family history.

The Apostle Paul makes it clear that Gentile believers are grafted into the family tree – we are adopted into the family of God through our faith in Jesus. Jesus' family is Israel, as represented by the Jews, and now with a further revelation that that salvation was to all nations who would worship and walk in faith in the one true Creator God revealed in the Old Covenant and manifested in the person of Jesus Christ. We cannot lay claim to the family inheritance and, at the same time, dissociate ourselves with the family name and history. We should not seek to bury it or deny it exists or hide that identity and those traditions simply because we don't want to be identified with our family inheritance. Doing so, in some sense, rejects who we are.[1]

But this is exactly what the Church did just a few hundred years after Christ's ascension. Sadly, the Gentile Church chose to separate itself from its root identity. A key step in the separation occurred when the Church chose to no longer connect the celebration of its chief Holy Day – the resurrection of Jesus Christ from the dead – with its original context of the Feast of Passover. This fateful decision had a serious knock-on effect over the succeeding centuries, such that most people today (including most Jews and Christians) would never see Christianity and Judaism as related, other than in the most rudimentary characteristics of what would be defined as a religion – for example, monotheism.

My hope is that this book will help Christians and Jews understand where their relationship with one another went out of order, and help Gentile believers consider the importance of repenting for rejecting their root identity and inheritance in Israel and the Old Covenant, especially through understanding and embracing the importance of God's Appointed Times in precipitating unified worship to the One True God – as manifested to us through the Father, Son and Holy Spirit. This is the God of the New and Old Covenants. My prayer is that this will help restore unity and result in a powerful move of the Holy Spirit in healing and restoring the Body of Jesus to its fullness of maturity and Holy Spirit empowerment as the One New Man.

I

Addressing Antisemitism

Before we begin considering the brokenness and healing needs of the One New Man and the importance of God's Appointed Times to that process, we need to address any influence of antisemitism in our own thinking.

The antisemitic spirit goes hand in hand with an antichrist spirit. It is passed from generation to generation as a curse that follows the family line and will cause all manner of destruction to the purposes of God in families, communities, and nations. If any antisemitic attitudes or beliefs exist in us or our family line that have not been dealt with before the Lord, we will either be offended, distracted, confused, or all three by any teaching on the topic of this book. An alternative reaction, if we haven't dealt with antisemitism, might be an openness to God's Appointed Times, but a tendency to become legalistic about them. Legalism is a subtle manifestation of the antichrist spirit. And the antichrist spirit is always, ultimately, antisemitic.

Over the last 15 years since the Lord revealed to me the

importance of God's Appointed Times and their current relevance to the Body of Christ, I have taught numerous groups of people about the feasts, just as the Lord said I would. But when I first began teaching these truths to my fellow believers, I quickly realized that I was not just dealing with ignorance of what the Bible had to say about these things. I was not wrestling with flesh and blood. Rather, I was battling spiritual forces that had specific assignments to keep God's people blinded to the truth about the feasts' importance and relevance to the Church.

I witnessed, in some of my initial teachings, people, whom I knew to be otherwise quite amiable, kind, loving, and gracious, suddenly become hostile and offended. I encountered accusations like: "you are trying to put us under the law", "that's the law, I'm under grace", "you're trying to make me Jewish", and "you're promoting legalism." In fact, I have never suggested that anyone *must* participate in the feasts. I simply shared how they represented Jesus and His atoning work of salvation for mankind. How could a believer be offended by that? I never suggested that anyone was required to observe or participate in the feasts. And yet, it was as if my words were going through some kind of distortion chamber.

I realized this at a conference on the One New Man three or four years into my efforts to share about the feasts. It was a small group of people, and I knew nearly all those in attendance. I knew all of them loved the Lord and were dedicated to His service. They were all Spirit filled and open to the leading of the Lord.

At a break in the meetings, one of the people I highly respected and felt was really desiring to understand more about Israel, the Jewish roots of the faith, and the Feasts of the Lord, came to me and shared that they were struggling with being able to even listen to the teaching. They said they were confused, and they were having pain in their forehead area. I immediately felt that we were dealing with a spirit of antisemitism and quickly led the person in some prayers of generational repentance and forgiveness. Then I took authority over any spirit of antisemitism or other spirit assigned to block the person's understanding regarding the feasts and directed it to leave in the name of Jesus. The person immediately felt relief in their spirit and in their head where they had felt pain and tension. They were then able to return to the meetings and absorb what was being taught.

Another challenge I've faced when teaching on the feasts or the One New Man has been people who are receptive to the teaching taking it to extremes with a legalistic approach, and judgement against those who do not "get it" or refuse to celebrate the feasts in the manner they believe is appropriate. Legalism in our approach to the feasts will only alienate the Body of Christ from God's truth about the feasts and ultimately entangle its subjects in an antichrist spirit which I've seen go so far as to bring a believer to deny the deity of Jesus.

In light of this, I've learned to start all of my teachings about the feasts with teaching and prayer into antisemitism before explaining the importance of the feasts to Christians. I have found that the audience is much less confused, offended, and distracted when I proceed in this way. In fact, on a number of occasions where attendees at my courses on this topic have missed the initial teaching and prayer time about antisemitism and have joined the class later, I've noticed those same students struggle with the teaching in a way that those who have prayed with me regarding antisemitism do not.

It is, therefore, essential that, even though this book is not primarily about Israel or antisemitism, we first discuss the matter of antisemitism before proceeding. The reality is that many, if not most, Christians deal with some level of antisemitism in their backgrounds. I have found that people can even be "pro-Israel" but still have an antisemitic spirit affecting them. In fact, I have discovered that many Jewish people also have an antisemitic spirit affecting them. At first glance, this may seem counterintuitive. How can a Jew be antisemitic?

I have witnessed many Jewish people infected by this spirit who are hostile to their heritage, either because of family issues, cultural offense with their own Jewish culture, or because of past persecution stemming from being Jewish. These things can cause Jews to be affected by an antisemitic spirit, and accordingly, struggle with teaching on God's Appointed Times and the One New Man.

In a related scenario, very religious Jews are so anti-Jesus that the antichrist spirit causes them to even oppose the State of Israel. In this sense, they are antisemitic, even though they consider themselves the only "real" Jews. They cannot be open to what God is doing with the restoration of the Jews to the land of Israel. In fact, some sects of ultra-orthodoxy oppose the existence of the State of Israel so much that they join anti-Israel protests. Many of the more extreme orthodox men in Israel refuse to serve in the Israeli army despite enjoying its protection.

Generational iniquity

In case you are unfamiliar with this truth, let me provide a brief explanation of generational iniquity. The Scriptures make clear that the sins of the fathers will be visited upon the children to the third and fourth generation (Deut. 5:9-10). In the ministry where I currently serve, we have witnessed literally hundreds and thousands of people set free from evil spirits that have been vexing them through the rights given the enemy through previous generations' sins. When that sin is brought to the Lord, confessed, renounced, and repented of, and the ancestors forgiven by the individual affected by the generational iniquity, the spirits operating through that platform of authority lose their authority to continue to operate in their life. Those spirits must then leave at the direction of any believer who is walking in the power of the Holy Spirit and the authority of the name of Jesus.

In fact, generational iniquity is the only root issue that affects nearly every individual with whom I have ministered. Generational iniquity doesn't force us to commit the same sins as our forefathers, nor is it to be used to avoid taking personal responsibility for our own sin. We must confess and repent of our own sins, whether they are generational in origin or not. But the fact remains that many people who suffer with various physical maladies, attractions to certain kinds of sin, or harassment by evil spirits in their thinking and behavior, have never personally committed the sin that is in their generational line which opened the doors to these issues. But it is a very real "door" for the enemy to enter and affect thinking, behavior, attitudes, and even physical functions. Generational iniquity sets up a "crookedness" or "distortion" in our thinking and behavior that influences us toward those beliefs and behaviors. We still have personal responsibility and ability to resist these temptations, but dealing with generational iniquity before the Lord will remove spiritual "pressure" towards those sins and help dispel unbiblical beliefs and thinking.

Two sources of antisemitism among non-Jews

An antisemitic spirit can have authority to operate in a believer's life through two different "generational lines." Typically, when we are discussing generational iniquity and related spiritual authority operating in a believer's life, we are referring to their physical family bloodline. And that is true in the case of antisemitism.

But with antisemitism, we have a second "generational line" that can be opening a door to a spirit of antisemitism operating on our thinking. This is our spiritual generational line. That is the "Church lineage" into which we have been born again. Just like our biological family, our church family has a spiritual DNA and that is passed on spiritually and by way of teaching and example in a manner similar to our biological family line. Just as in our biological family, our spiritual family into which we were born again can pass along both truth and error through their beliefs, teachings, and actions.

In the context of antisemitism, the Bible is clear that God blesses those that bless Jacob (Israel) and his offspring, and He curses those that curse them. One of the greatest curses anyone can experience is blindness to the things of God. We cannot know truth without revelation. Jesus is Truth. Thank God that He is merciful and gives us many chances to know and hear His voice and to correct our ways. The Spirit of Truth, who is the Spirit of Jesus, is operating even now to bring truth and light! Antisemitism causes spiritual blindness to God's plans and purposes for the Church and Israel.

Generational sin in our biological family line

Antisemitism in our biological family line exists in many people groups who come from a European background, including: Eastern and Western Europe, the United States, South America, Australia, and South Africa. Similarly, most, if not all, individuals of Arab and other non-Jewish middle eastern decent must face the almost certain reality of antisemitism in their physical DNA.

All these groups have a history of hostility towards the Jewish people, as well as a long history of fighting over the land of Israel and attempting to defeat God's purposes for the Jews in that land. In fact, many of us can recall off-color jokes, ridicule, cursing and other expressions of antisemitism in our immediate families. In the southern United States, for instance, most Caucasians must deal with racism in their family lines that included antisemitism. Many southerners' ancestors were involved in organizations like the Ku Klux Klan and Freemasonry. These organizations encourage and teach both antichrist and antisemitic behaviors and beliefs. All of this must be dealt with before the Lord if we have never addressed this generational iniquity in our family of origin.

Generational sin in our spiritual family line

Antisemitism in our "spiritual family" is often more subtle. Sadly, most of the Church is unaware that it has been infected by anti-semitism. Replacement Theology entered the Church in its earliest days and argues that believers in Jesus – now called The Church – replace Israel in all the promises of God in the Old and New Testament. The theory is that Israel had one chance to get it right when Jesus came, and they rejected Him. Therefore, God has no purposes for them in the future and they are replaced in God's eternal plan by Christians. This theology resulted in many Christians partaking in shedding Jewish blood and treating the Jewish people in the most abominable way. Hitler's holocaust was a direct result of this theology, and it was how many European Christians justified their treatment of the Jews, from the Crusades, to the pogroms in Russia, to the Spanish Inquisition, to the direct or indirect participation in the Holocaust.

Most evangelicals do not hold to Replacement Theology and would argue vehemently that they are not antisemitic. However, even though the evangelical movement has been largely pro-Israel since World War II, their theology belies their words. Indeed, in the last decade, we have seen a significant and alarming shift among evangelical believers to positions that claim to be only "anti-Israel" but not antisemitic. They have been deceived into believing that the destiny of the Jewish people (and of believers in Jesus, for that matter) is not directly related to God's purposes for Israel and the Jewish people in the land that He promised to them. But the two cannot be separated. God's purposes for the descendants of Jacob (the Jewish people) and the land of Israel are inextricably connected.

Moreover, because antisemitism has not been confronted and

confessed by the Church, theological distortion and error still influence the Evangelical Church and its theology. As explained in more detail in other chapters, the roots of antisemitism date back to the second century Church fathers' teachings and culminated in a breaking of the identity of the Church as rooted in Israel and the Old Covenant. This was formalized at the Council of Nicaea and succeeding Church councils. But these attitudes, beliefs, and resulting theologies continue to infect the Church today – even in the part of the Church that claims not to adopt "Replacement Theology."

For instance, headings in the Old Testament Bible I used in my Evangelical Church and Bible college as a child and young man implied that promises to Israel and the Jewish people in the Old Testament prophetic books like Isaiah and Jeremiah were promises to the (now almost exclusively) Gentile Christian Church.

Similarly, eschatological teaching in the Evangelical Church largely promotes a belief that all believers in Jesus will exit the earth before any Jews begin to turn to their Messiah in any significant way. This belief not only causes believers to see the Jews as "unsaveable" – at least in our time – and undermines efforts to reach them with the Gospel, but it relieves us from any responsibility to support the Jewish people in their efforts to survive. A sort of Calvinistic predestination attitude induces a "spiritual lethargy" in the Church's approach to its relationship with the Jewish people and the land of Israel. And it avoids the Church's responsibility and calling to be instrumental in bringing the Jewish people back to their Messiah – the place and person of true worship. In a word, it undermines the realization of the One New Man.

On this note, if the One New Man was not to be genuinely realized until Jesus' Millennial reign, why did the Apostle Paul spend so much time trying to help us understand how to get along as Jewish and Gentile believers? If the Millennial reign must ensue before the

One New Man can be realized in any significant way, why would Paul be encouraging understanding and humility in navigating the relationship? After all, in the Millennium, the lion and lamb will lie down together. It seems like a foregone conclusion that Jewish and Gentile believers will be unified then.

The truth is that the Lord meant for these things to culminate before His Second Coming. Admittedly, the full realization of the One New Man cannot occur until Jesus rules and reigns on the earth, but the Scriptures are clear that the Jews will turn to the Lord immediately before Jesus' return, and that Gentile believers are to be instrumental in that process.

These and other teachings and prejudices expressed by the early Church fathers as further elaborated on in Chapter 6 demonstrate that antisemitism is part of most, if not all, believers' spiritual family inheritance. Indeed, all of the Church reformers were vitriolically antisemitic.

Dealing with the spirit of antisemitism

How do we deal with antisemitism in both our biological and spiritual generational line? The steps to freedom from the influence of this spirit are the same as with any generational sin: bring the antisemitism before the Lord, confess it as sin (meaning agree with the Lord that it is/was sin), renounce any antisemitic attitudes, words, or behavior, and repent of it (that is, turn away from it and commit not to return to it), ask forgiveness for your personal antisemitism and that of your family line, forgive your ancestors for opening that door and the effect it has had on you, your family and any children you have had. Finally, in the name of Jesus, simply tell any spirits that have been operating through that platform of authority in your life or that of your family line to leave and not return. Invite God to fill you with His truth. Share what you've done with another believer who you know walks according to the Spirit.

I would encourage you, before proceeding further in this book, to turn to Appendix 1 and pray through the prayers outlined there. Pray through these prayers even if you don't know or believe that you have any antisemitism in your biological family background or church heritage. In fact, I would encourage everyone to also pray the prayers related to those who have a Jewish background. I have found that many people in the Church have a Jewish background that has been either rejected or of which they are not fully aware, and this hinders them from embracing the fullness of the Gospel as rooted in Israel and the Old Covenant. Please don't skip praying through Appendix 1. It is an essential step before attempting to digest the rest of this book.

2

A Revelation

Now that we have dealt with any strongholds of the enemy that block our ability to consider the importance of Israel, the Old Covenant, and the Feasts of the Lord to a Christian, let me share a bit of my story as to why I have been compelled to teach on this subject. This part of my story begins in 2009 and the setting is Blackpool, England.

"Why am I here?" This question reverberated through my mind as I sat in the closing session of a four-day conference. It was not the broader esoteric question about the meaning of life or human existence in space and time. No, my question was much more practical. Why was I sitting in a hotel conference room in Blackpool, England, on a cold, dreary winter day?

To be honest, I was a little irritated with the Lord. He had given me such a strong impression that I was to attend the conference and that I should ask my wife, Becky, to accompany me. The fact that she said "yes" and now stood beside me as we sang the words of a familiar worship song in a rather dilapidated hotel in

Blackpool, England, on that Saturday morning in early 2009 was a small miracle. Her willingness to leave our two young children with friends while we traveled across the Atlantic felt like confirmation to me that attending this conference was important and that the Lord must have something significant to impart to us through our attendance.

But, sitting there on Saturday morning, the last day of the conference, I found myself asking God: "What's the point?" The teachings we had heard were certainly good, but we could have listened to that information in the comfort of our home or office in Florida via some form of digital media. Why was it necessary for us to be at this conference during the most miserable time of the year in a place like Blackpool, England, far from our children, home, and ministry responsibilities? Even the immigration officer at Manchester Airport grimaced and expressed his sympathy when I related our intended destination.

As I stood there contemplating these questions and having an internal conversation with the Lord about my disappointment, I found my mind wandering to the flight home, and to getting on with my many responsibilities as a pastor on staff at a rapidly growing church in the suburbs of Tampa, Florida. The theme of the conference we were attending, entitled "Arise" – based on Isaiah 60:1, involving Israel and God's eternal purposes and covenant with that nation and people – seemed largely irrelevant to my daily ministry and life back in Florida.

Don't misunderstand. I cared about Israel; or at least, I thought I did. I had grown up in a conservative evangelical denomination, and had heard from my earliest years that God was not finished with Israel. He had an eternal purpose and covenant with His chosen people. I had largely been insulated from Replacement Theology. But, in practical terms, my Christian upbringing had included very little guidance on how these beliefs about Israel and the Jewish people related to my relationship with Jesus in 2009.

In fact, based on my education through the churches in which I grew up and the Bible college where I completed my theological training, I believed that someday, in the distant future, the Jewish people and the nation of Israel would turn *en masse* and believe in Jesus (or Yeshua, as His name is pronounced in Hebrew)[2]. These events, however, were always described as happening sometime when I, as a Christian, had departed the earth via the rapture. Thus, in practical terms, the outworking of my beliefs in God's purposes for Israel resulted in no tangible action on my part. I might have a conversation with someone from time to time about supporting Israel as a nation, but there was no real practical outworking to my favorable disposition toward Israel. After all, if this was God's divine plan to be implemented after I'm long gone, what responsibility or impact could I have on the process of its implementation?

Perhaps these thoughts did not all formulate in this exact way that fateful Saturday morning, but they nevertheless were influencing my mental "check-out" from the conference back to the practical daily matters of ministry. Still, I couldn't help but feel a bit disappointed that something more significant hadn't materialized at the conference. I had felt such a strong prompting by the Holy Spirit that I was to be there. Maybe I hadn't heard the Lord correctly . . .

So began the final message of the conference, presented by the founder of Ellel Ministries – the organization sponsoring the conference. The speaker chose for his text Romans chapter 11. I do not recall the message in any detail. But as the message progressed, the Lord began to illuminate the words of Romans 11 to my mind and spirit like never before. As I read the words the Apostle Paul penned in Romans 11:11-12, it was as if I saw the words for the first time:

"Again I ask: Did they [the Jews] stumble so as to fall beyond recovery? *Not at all!* Rather, because of their transgression, salvation has come to the Gentiles to make Israel envious. But if their transgression means riches for the world, and their loss means riches for the Gentiles, how much greater riches will their full inclusion bring!" (NIV 2011) (emphasis added)

And then a few verses later, Paul reiterates:

"For if their rejection brought reconciliation to the world, what will their acceptance *be but life from the dead?*" (NIV 2011) (emphasis added)

Although I had read these Scriptures many times in the past, it was as if I had never fully grasped their meaning. Lights were beginning to come on. The Holy Spirit was speaking to me:

"If the Gentiles have received salvation because the eyes of the people of Israel have been blinded to the truth of who I was and had thus, as a people, rejected Me as their Messiah for a period of time, their general acceptance of Me as Messiah isn't just going to mean another revival. No, it will be a revival to end all revivals. All previous moves of the Holy Spirit will pale in comparison to when large numbers of Jewish people recognize Me for who I Am – it will be like watching resurrection from the dead."

My mind raced through all I had come to know about the great accomplishments of the Jewish people in every sector of life and society – all the great inventors, authors, scientists, teachers, politicians, and entertainers. When these people recognize Yeshua as Messiah and take on their God-ordained role as a priestly nation and the role of the first born in God's reconciling work on the earth, there will be no stopping the tidal wave of the Kingdom of God coming in its fullness on earth.

These thoughts and many others exploded across my mind. The Lord was illuminating these Scriptures to me like never before. I was experiencing what Messianic teacher and author Peter Tsukahira calls "the penny dropping" with regard to my understanding of God's heart and purposes for Israel and the Jewish people. I raced on through the passage, excited to see what else the Apostle Paul had to say.

It wasn't until sometime later, when I reflected on what had happened, that it occurred to me that I had read the book of Romans numerous times before that day, but had never really comprehended these words. They certainly had never had the impact on my thoughts and imagination like they did that cold Saturday morning of early 2009 in Blackpool, England.

But the Lord wasn't done speaking to me that morning. As I was trying to digest the fresh understanding the Lord was giving me, I sped on past the text of the message and into chapter twelve of Romans. The Lord was speaking to me in a nearly audible voice now:

> Therefore, I urge you, brothers and sisters, in view of God's mercy, to offer your bodies as a living sacrifice, holy and pleasing to God—this is your true and proper worship. Do not conform to the pattern of this world, but be transformed by the renewing of your mind. Then you will be able to test and approve what God's will is—his good, pleasing and perfect will. (Romans 12:1-2) (NIV)

The words I had heard so many times in the past about Biblical interpretation sprang to my mind: "If you see the words, 'wherefore' or 'therefore', you need to consider what they are there for." In other words, when you see these terms, look to what precedes them, because that is the reason for the words that will follow.

As I pondered this, I realized that I had heard numerous messages preached on Romans 12:1. Many of them were "missions" messages used to encourage Christians to reach the nations with the Gospel – sacrificially giving and going to far-flung locations so that the whole world might hear the good news of Jesus. But I had never heard anyone connect the words of Romans 12:1 to the chapters immediately preceding it and Paul's lengthy discussion from Roman 9 through 11 regarding Israel's acceptance of Jesus as Messiah and the ramifications for the world of that development. Now the implications of Romans 12 became starkly related to Paul's discussion of the interplay between the people of Israel and God's covenant with them, and God's purposes in also making a way for the Gentiles to be saved and reconciled to Himself. In fact, these words are directly related to Paul's admonition in Romans 11 to Gentile believers that they provoke Israel to jealousy.

What Paul was saying is simply this: "Therefore – because of this amazing thing God is working out with reconciling the Gentiles to Himself and then bringing the people of Israel back to Himself – we need to give ourselves sacrificially for these purposes and then let God transform our minds so that we can understand what His will is for us in helping to bring this to pass in our given season serving Him on this earth."

But the Lord was bringing these thoughts from a general application to the Church to a very specific application for me. In my spirit, I heard the Lord say: "Matt, I want you to present yourself to Me to be used for My special purposes related to the people and nation of Israel." He didn't explain what this meant in practical terms, but the words and direction were clear. He wanted me to follow Him and do His bidding to be an instrument for the people and nation of Israel to come to their fullness of purpose in His Kingdom.

Of course, these words from the Lord prompted several additional questions. But the immediate word from the Lord was clear, and His invitation inescapable. He wanted me to present myself to Him for His purposes related to Israel – and do it immediately. In a real sense, He was saying, "Arise and follow Me in helping Me implement My purposes for the people and nation of Israel and the Body of Christ."

As the speaker began his conclusion, I tuned back in just in time to hear him say that they were going to take up an offering to support the launch of Ellel Ministries' work in Israel. He said they were going to place a sheet out in front of the platform, and he was inviting people to put their offering for Israel in the sheet. As he spoke these words, the Lord said: "Matt, I want you to put yourself in the sheet."

I immediately began to resist. "Lord," I said in my heart, "what will people think? These people don't know me. They'll think I'm getting in the offering to steal some of it. I can't kneel in the sheet. Even if they believe You are telling me to kneel in the sheet where the offerings are being placed, this is completely inappropriate for England. Everyone is very proper here. What will they think of some American with a wild notion that God told him to kneel in the offering sheet?" My arguments apparently had no effect on the Holy Spirit. In fact, the more I argued, the stronger the urging of the Lord became.

As the conviction grew stronger, people began to take their funds to the sheet. I got out my wallet and began to fumble with some bills. The Lord said clearly: "Matt, I don't want your money, I want you. Go kneel in the sheet." In a last-ditch effort to dissuade the Lord, I prayed: "If this is really you Lord, please tell my wife." I glanced to my left at my wife who had her head down and her eyes closed. I felt I should ask her to go with me, but figured she would say yes even if she did have reservations because she is just that kind of wife – always ready to support me even if she does think I'm crazy!

So I waited for her to make a move. The conviction continued but lifted as the opportunity to act passed. I had not obeyed the Lord's directive to kneel in the sheet, but I did understand the implications of the action He had wanted me to take, and I had made the commitment in my heart to do whatever the Lord wanted me to do related to Israel.

As the service concluded, I had to repent of my questioning the Lord for having me attend the conference. Now I understood the reason for my presence there. It was a God-ordained moment between me, the Lord and, as I would find out later, my wife. In the waning moments of the conference, the Lord placed a deep understanding and a profound call on my future that I could not ignore. Although my question regarding why I was at the conference had been answered, that answer raised even more questions.

I also had to repent for my disobedience in not going forward to kneel in the sheet. It wouldn't be the last time I would question God or question whether I was hearing God correctly. Since that morning, these sorts of questions have come many times. I suppose this has always been the nature of walking with the Lord. Many times, there are more questions than answers. But this does not excuse us from taking the next step the Lord is asking us to take. As the return of the Lord rapidly approaches, we must learn to hear His voice and when we know He is speaking, and we are clear on what He is saying to do, we must not hesitate to act. (Of course, we must always test these promptings against God's written Word to guard ourselves against deception.)

So began a significant new season in my life. A season of pursuing just what the Lord meant by the impressions He had given me regarding advancing His Kingdom purposes related to the people and nation of Israel. What did all this mean for me personally? But, more importantly, what did these revelations the Lord had given me about the importance of understanding the relationship of Israel and the Gentile Church mean to the broader Body of Christ?

3

What Next?

We had a flight booked the following morning from Manchester International Airport to Orlando, Florida, and so we needed to catch a train from Blackpool to Manchester immediately after the conference ended. As we rode to the train station, my head was reeling with the implications of the download I had just received from the Lord.

After boarding the train, my wife sat across from me as we made our way toward Manchester. We sat in silence for some time – each in our own world, considering all we had heard and seen during the last few days. As we neared our destination station, I finally shared what I felt the Lord had asked me to do during the time the offering was being taken in the last session of the conference. Becky listened intently and appeared to want to respond, but an interruption cut our conversation short.

A few days later, when we had regained some semblance of normalcy at home in Florida, we had an opportunity to talk at length about what had transpired while we were in England. It was then that my wife shared with me what she had experienced during the time the offering was being taken the previous Saturday morning. While she had her head bowed and her eyes closed, and while the Lord was telling me to "go kneel in the sheet," she had a vision. Her vision was of me kneeling in the collection sheet!

Despite my reservations and my failure to obey the Lord's directive to kneel in the sheet, He had answered my prayer that I had whispered during that time, asking Him to confirm the word He was giving me about Israel and to kneel in the sheet. He had in fact confirmed what He had spoken into my heart by giving my wife a vision at the same moment He was speaking to me.

This confirmed to me that the Lord had some special purpose He wanted me to pursue related to Israel. But what did it mean in practical terms? What was the next step? Was I to leave my pastoral position and go to Israel in some role? Was I to further my education? Who could I talk to about these things?

I began wrestling through these questions with the Lord in prayer. Again and again, I found myself asking God how to move forward with the word He had given me. I felt I needed to do *something*, but I had no idea where to start. So I prayed.

It was during this season of seeking the Lord that I first encountered the significant attack and oppression of the enemy that comes when one attempts to pursue anything related to the Kingdom of God and Israel. It shouldn't have been a surprise to me, considering the importance of Israel to the Lord and His Kingdom. But it was something I had never experienced before. So at first, I didn't relate it to the calling God had given me regarding Israel.

One morning in early March of 2009, just a little over a month after my experience in Blackpool, I found myself oppressed by the enemy to such a degree that I felt physically sick. I knew I was not physically ill, but I felt so negative and heavy that I didn't feel I could even get up to go into my office at the church. Words of accusation and negative thoughts about myself and my ministry plagued my mind.

I have been blessed with good health and have seldom called in sick to work, but that morning I could not muster the strength to face anyone or anything. I called the church office and told them I would not be in that morning. After I hung up the phone, the negative accusations continued to flood my mind and all I could really do was pray.

Someone has said that when under serious attack from the enemy our short prayer should be "Help!" and our long prayer should be "Help, Lord!" I alternated between these two prayers throughout the morning. That morning, I also wrestled with the Lord about the things He had spoken to me about Israel. What did it mean? What was I supposed to do with it?

That same day, the senior pastor at the church where I served as an associate pastor had an appointment scheduled with a Messianic Jewish believer who was going to help our church hold a Passover Seder.[3] This would be the first Passover Seder that we had ever held at our church. The senior pastor had invited me to the planning meeting if I wanted to attend. But the way I was feeling that morning, I had no intention of participating in any meeting.

At about 11 a.m., I received a call from the church. The senior pastor had something pressing come up and would be unable to attend the Seder planning meeting. He asked me to take the meeting for him. Still feeling the heavy grey cloud of oppression, I grudgingly told the senior pastor's assistant that I would be in shortly. I got up and began to get ready. My strength seemed to rally as I dressed and made my way to the church.

In retrospect, all the oppression made sense, because it was during that meeting the Lord gave me an answer to my question: "What next?" As we sat discussing the Seder, I began to share what I felt the Lord had spoken to me in Blackpool. As we talked, the Lord spoke very clearly to me: "Matt, you don't have to know everything about the implications of what I spoke to you in Blackpool. For now, just begin by visiting Israel and starting Hebrew lessons."

What a relief! I didn't have to figure it all out or lay out a master plan. I didn't have to quit my job and move to Israel. I just had to take these two simple steps – study Hebrew; visit Israel. Coincidentally, the lady I met with that day taught Hebrew classes, and I found a ministry tour to Israel scheduled for June that I felt I should join. I had my first two assignments.

I was excited about what the future held, and I felt like I had some direction regarding the next steps to take. The months that followed were full of new revelation. To those in the Messianic movement and those who have studied the Jewish roots of the faith, all of these things I was learning would be considered yesterday's news. But for me, it was fresh revelation that had been "hiding" in the Scriptures my whole life, waiting to be revealed to me by the Lord when my heart was ready to receive it.

I read through the book of Romans three times in ten days during my first visit to Israel in the summer of 2009. I began to see the book of Romans as more of a practical handbook on how Jewish and Gentile believers should understand and treat each other, rather than a theological commentary on the doctrine of election. At its core, Romans is a guidebook for how Jewish and Gentile believers are to get along with one another – an exhortation to respect one another's value and purpose in the Kingdom while maintaining our own unique identities as Jews and Gentiles. I was beginning to formulate an understanding of the "one new man" Paul talked about in Ephesians 2:15. Slowly, my mind was beginning to be renewed and my thinking was being transformed in many ways. Along with this new revelation regarding God's purposes and plans for Israel and their inextricable link to His work in the Gentiles, the Lord was taking me on a parallel track of healing and restoration. He was giving me a new understanding of the Kingdom of God and the fullness of the Messianic purposes of Jesus as prophesied in Isaiah 61 and quoted by the Lord Jesus in Luke 4.

The Lord was removing my ignorance, blindness, and hardness of heart toward things of the Kingdom, particularly on issues related to the people and nation of Israel. I thought I had always supported God's purposes for Israel and His chosen people. I thought I had always understood the fullness of the Gospel. But I was now realizing that there were many things I had been missing.

As I stood looking over the Valley of Megiddo from Mt. Carmel during that first trip to Israel, the Spirit of the Lord was so intensely moving on me that I thought I might completely lose my composure if He didn't relent. When I prayed at the Western Wall for what seemed to me to be only five minutes, the time with the Lord was so intense that the five minutes I perceived had passed was closer to one hour.

Through the late summer and early fall of 2009, the Lord prompted me to read Leviticus and Deuteronomy. I began to see the meaning of the Scriptures as they were written in their original context and language. Scriptures I had simply glossed over in the past because of lack of understanding or boredom, now had significance. I began to read with an intentionality for understanding these Old Testament passages and the reason for their inclusion in God's Word.

Rather than forging on in my Bible reading when the passages seemed irrelevant to my life, or running to a commentary to have someone else tell me the meaning or purpose of the passage, I began to dwell on the Scripture till I received understanding. Often, I would simply stop on a chapter or part of a chapter that I did not understand, re-reading it over and over while asking the Lord for illumination, waiting to move on until the Lord gave me understanding by the Holy Spirit.

In some ways, very quickly, and in other ways excruciatingly slowly, the Lord was tearing down and rebuilding my understanding of His Kingdom and my role in it. The mosaic of His greater plans and purposes became exceedingly vast, and my part in those vast plans began to become clearer.

I began to see that God's calling for me was twofold: 1) to help believers come to healing and wholeness in their body, soul, and spirit and, by so doing, 2) to help the Church prepare to usher in the next great move of God - the turning of the people of Israel to Messiah – and the realization of the fullness of the "One New Man" in Messiah that Paul references in Ephesians.

Over time, I began to recognize that the healing ministry and the realization of the "One New Man" are not separate and distinct issues in the Kingdom. Healing and restoration of individuals is indispensable to the realization of the "One New Man" and the realization of the unity of the "One New Man" will release the Kingdom purposes of God in healing and restoration of individuals like we haven't seen since the events recorded in the Book of Acts. Healing and the realization of the "One New Man" are two sides of a single coin – inextricably connected. One is the key to the other.

4

The One New Man

During the preparation for my first conference on the One New Man, I received a call from an interested party. Her question surprised me. She wanted to know if the conference was applicable to women as well as men. I found this question very telling because it revealed a major problem. It demonstrated how relatively rarely the topic of the One New Man is discussed in the mainstream Church.

My quick search of Amazon at the time of the writing of this book revealed only 12 books with titles related to "The One New Man". In the last 20 years, a growing number of teachings on the subject have been published. But the amount of writing and teaching on the topic in the Church is still relatively small compared to many other theological topics. Moreover, the themes of many of these books focus on the topic of unity of Gentile believers – that is, breaking down walls among denominations within the Gentile church or between the Gentile races. Relatively few focus on the relationship of the Church to the Jewish people and the nation of Israel.

The phrase "one new man" is found in chapter 2 of Paul's Epistle to the Ephesians. Specifically, Ephesians 2:11-17 says:

> Wherefore remember, that once ye, the Gentiles in the flesh, who are called Uncircumcision by that which is called Circumcision, in the flesh, made by hands; that ye were at that time separate from Christ, alienated from the commonwealth of Israel, and strangers from the covenants of the promise, having no hope and without God in the world. But now in Christ Jesus ye that once were far off are made nigh in the blood of Christ. For he is our peace, who made both one, and brake down the middle wall of partition, having abolished in his flesh the enmity, *even* the law of commandments *contained* in ordinances; that he might create in himself of the two **one new man**, *so* making peace; and might reconcile them both in one body unto God through the cross, having slain the enmity thereby: and he came and preached peace to you that were far off, and peace to them that were nigh . . . . (emphasis added) (ASV)

It is clear from the context of this Scripture that the primary focus of any book on the One New Man should be on the relationship between Jew and Gentile. Any discussion of the passage has to first deal with the oneness Paul describes between Jew and Gentile – not just between believing Gentiles.

In our recent past as a Church, very few people even mentioned the issue, let alone did any significant study on the outworking of the concept. Indeed, it seemed somewhat irrelevant because the Jewish character of Christianity had faded significantly, and few

Jews were coming to faith. However, since the regathering of Israel to her ancient homeland and the re-formation of the modern State of Israel – and particularly in the years since 1967 when Jerusalem came back under Jewish control for the first time since Jerusalem's destruction by Rome in 70 AD – many Jews have been born again and have been led to identify themselves as Jews who believe in Jesus as Messiah, *i.e.*, Messianic Jews. This in turn has challenged the theology of the predominantly Gentile church and the practical outworking of our faith. Indeed, Jewish believers in Messiah have helped bring Gentiles back to the Jewish roots of their Christian faith.

In addition to the move of God on the hearts of Jewish people to bring them to acceptance of Jesus as their Messiah, a movement of the Holy Spirit is afoot among Gentile believers. In my discussions with people across the Church in various denominations over the past several years since my encounter with the Lord in 2009, when He opened my eyes about Israel, it has become obvious that the Lord is doing something supernatural. He's bringing the Gentile Church back to this most important Kingdom principle of unity – especially as it relates to Israel and the Jewish people and their relationship with the Church.

Just as Jews are being supernaturally drawn to their Messiah and the New Covenant in His blood, so are born-again, Spirit filled, Gentile believers being drawn back to the Old Covenant foundations of their New Covenant faith. These developments have created a unique challenge for the Church that it has not faced for nearly 2000 years. How do the Old Covenant commands of God to Israel fit with the New Covenant practices we Gentiles have developed over the past 18 centuries, largely bereft of Jewish and Old Covenant influence?

Despite some major advancements in the realization of a truly "One New Man" body of believers made up of both Jews and

Gentiles, vast divisions seem to remain within the body of Messiah. The divide between the two seems too great to bridge. There seems to be a barrier that we are unable to fully overcome to realize the unity that Jesus prayed for as recorded in John 17 right before He went to the cross.

But in the last two decades, I believe the Lord has been revealing to the church some important keys to realizing the unity He so fervently prayed for in the Garden and for which He now intercedes before the Father.

From a medical perspective, in order to bring physical healing or restoration to a person, there are several things that we commonly need to consider. We first need to study the original design for the body – how the different parts are to interact with one another and how they should function in their original condition. Second, we need to consider how the body went out of order. Third, we need to deliberate on how to best put the various parts back into order. Fourth, we must take the physical action to place the body in order. Finally, we must seek the Lord for His healing work. Because all healing comes from the Lord, physicians can place the body of an accident victim back in as close to proper order as possible, the body must then perform its healing functions as designed, and the Lord, as Divine Healer, must be invited into that process.

In the healing ministry, I have witnessed people who have been injured in an accident struggle with physical healing after an accident even if it has been put back the way it should be by physicians. Sometimes, the body still will not heal. There seems to be some kind of blockage to the natural healing process. We have found that the process of healing may be hindered or prevented because of disorder within the person's soul or spirit. Because we are three parts – body, soul, and spirit – disorder in one part can potentially affect the other parts. When I have helped the person deal with the spiritual and/or emotional issues that are blocking the physical healing, the body then proceeds with its normal processes of healing.

In the same way, the One New Man cannot heal properly and become unified in the way the Lord intends if we do not deal with the brokeness and blockages to healing that came into the Body of Christ during its "childhood." Thus, in order to bring healing to the One New Man, we must consider the blueprint God has for the Body of Christ. We must then consider where things went out of order. Finally, we must consider what keys and truths can bring restoration to the disorder.

32 ~ MATTHEW MOORE

5

God's Design for the Church

There is little argument among Christian theologians that the Body of Christ is synonymous with what we now call "The Church." So there will be no confusion, throughout this book, when I use the term "Church," I am referring not to a building or denomination, but to that group of people that have placed their personal trust and faith in Jesus for their salvation. They are trusting in Him and Him alone for their salvation and are in no way relying upon their works of righteousness. Despite their varied denominational and church practices, this group of individuals is universally agreed that salvation is by grace through faith in Jesus and the work He did upon the Cross as a substitutionary atonement for their sins. They must make a personal decision to put their faith in Jesus. They are not part of the Church simply because their parents attended or were part of a church. Salvation is not by denominational affiliation or any particular religious activity, but because of their personal faith in Jesus. And they are marked as a believer by the indwelling Holy Spirit.

Although I use the term "Church" for this group of people, I note that the word "Church" is not a proper translation of the Greek word used and translated "Church" in the Authorized and many other versions of the Scripture. The word translated "Church" is the Greek word *ekklesia* which should have been translated "assembly." (As a side note, it is interesting that the references to the Children of Israel who entered into a covenant with the Lord at Mt. Sinai were referred to repeatedly as the "assembly.")

So I use the Church here out of convenience to refer to the universal body of those who have made a personal faith decision to follow Jesus Christ. I do not believe, nor do I assume, that any single Christian denomination is the Church. But most, if not all, Christian denominations contain at least a remnant of born-again believers that are The Church.

This Church is the Body of Christ as Paul references many times in his writings. He emphasized over and over the need for unity of the Body and respect for all parts of the Body of Christ. Unfortunately, Paul's exhortations have gone largely unheeded or at least unrealized.

It is in this context that we consider the original plan for Christ's body. It seems clear from the prayers of Jesus in the garden, to the writings of Paul, to the behavior of the early Church, that the Lord's original plan did not involve what we now know as denominationalism. At least, He certainly could not have intended for there to be the kind of rancor that exists between denominations. Even among "true" believers within these denominations, there seems to be disunity that the Lord clearly never intended.

In John 17:11 and 21-23, Jesus prayed:

> I will remain in the world no longer, but they are still

in the world, and I am coming to you. Holy Father, protect them by the power of your name, the name you gave me, so that they may be one as we are one . . . . My prayer is not for them alone. I pray also for those who will believe in me through their message, that all of them may be one, Father, just as you are in me and I am in you. May they also be in us so that the world may believe that you have sent me. I have given them the glory that you gave me, that they may be one as we are one— I in them and you in me—so that they may be brought to complete unity. Then the world will know that you sent me and have loved them even as you have loved me. (NIV)

Notice that the Lord repeats three times His prayer for the oneness of all believers. He prays for the oneness of those that believed in Him while He was still on the earth, but also for those who would believe in Him through the testimony and message of those existing believers. In other words, He was praying for us.

Jesus also goes far beyond our human ambitions for unity. When we create an organization, we are generally content to see the members of the organization be in agreement over a few main points for which the organization stands. Here, Jesus actually prays that believers will be one as He and the Father are one. This is a deep spiritual unity.

Jesus did only what the Father said to do. Jesus was praying for this same unity between us and Him and between us and one another. That kind of unity can't be accomplished by good programs, or by creative human organizational efforts. It can only be accomplished by the fullness of the reign of the Holy Spirit in all believers' lives. It is only the Spirit of Jesus Who can bring that type of unity. This kind of unity plainly does not leave room for denominational divisiveness that looks condescendingly on others who do not follow the same worship practices or who do not have identical theological beliefs.

Additionally, Paul's teaching in his epistles to the Corinthians and the Ephesians leaves no room for doubt on his position regarding divisiveness over dissimilar worship practices. Although Paul is uncompromising about maintaining the theological purity of the Gospel message, he shows little regard for the elevation of individual teachers to the kind of denominational division the Church has seen over the last several hundred years.

There is no support for the proposition that the Apostles (the founders of the New Testament Church) promoted the idea of division based on following a particular person's teachings. In fact, Paul, in his first epistle to the Church at Corinth, strongly condemned the idea of believers elevating one individual teacher or church leader over another saying:

> What then is Apollos? and what is Paul? Ministers through whom ye believed; and each as the Lord gave to him. I planted, Apollos watered; but God gave the increase. So then neither is he that plant[s] anything, neither he that water[s]; but God that giveth the increase. Now he that plant[s] and he that water[s] are one: but each shall receive his own reward according to his own labor. For we are God's fellow-workers: ye are God's husbandry, God's building. I Cor. 3:5-9 (ASV)

Nor does He recognize a place for condescension toward differing worship expressions of faith in Jesus – namely the celebration of certain holy days, ceremonies, and celebrations. For he states:

> Therefore do not let anyone judge you by what you eat or drink, or with regard to a religious festival, a New Moon celebration or a Sabbath day. These are a shadow of the things that were to come; the reality, however, is found in Christ. Do not let anyone who delights in false humility and the worship of angels disqualify you. Such a person also goes into great detail about what they have seen; they are puffed up with idle notions by their unspiritual mind. They have lost connection with the head, from whom the whole body, supported and held together by its ligaments and sinews, grows as God causes it to grow. (Colossians 2:16-19) (NIV)

These words leave little doubt that the Apostles and early One New Man strived for a unified body that also allowed for individual creativity in expression of that faith.

Finally, the example of the early Church refutes any argument in support of the divisive denominational rancor that has marked the Christian Church since before the time of the Reformation. For example, in the early Church, there was no identification of the body of believers according to some denominational belief.

The only references to identifiable groups within the Church had to do with geography. For example, The Book of Acts mentions the Church at Jerusalem:

> Acts 8:1 – On that day a great persecution broke out against **the church in Jerusalem**, and all except the apostles were scattered throughout Judea and Samaria. Godly men buried Stephen and mourned deeply for him. But Saul began to destroy the church. (NIV) (emphasis added)

Acts 11:21 – News of this reached *the church in Jerusalem*, and they sent Barnabas to Antioch. (NIV) (emphasis added)

Similarly, in Acts 20:17 Paul is said to have summoned the Elders of the church at Ephesus: And from Miletus he sent to *Ephesus*, and called to him the elders of *the church*. (NIV) (emphasis added)

In I Cor. 1:2, Paul also addressed the "church of God in Corinth." (NIV) Thus, all these references point to recognition of a single body of believers separated only by geographic realities.

This way of looking at the assembly of believers that followed Yeshua as Messiah and Lord was in spite of rabbinical tradition. The more culturally normal way of identifying a Jew's religious affiliation in those days would have been to identify with the rabbi he followed.

Yet the only Rabbi that the early Church identified with was THE Rabbi, Yeshua. They were otherwise identified by region.

The Lord Himself in the book of Revelation recognized churches only by geographic location:

On the Lord's Day I was in the Spirit, and I heard behind me a loud voice like a trumpet, which said: "Write on a scroll what you see and send it to the seven churches: to Ephesus, Smyrna, Pergamum, Thyatira, Sardis, Philadelphia, and Laodicea. Rev. 1:10-11 (NIV)

Clearly the Lord's intention was not to institute His body divided by theological doctrines or forms of worship expression, but, at most, by geographic regions. In fact, the greatest theological schism at the time was with the Judaizers, who claimed that Gentiles had to be circumcised in order to be grafted in to the One New Man. This works-based theology of salvation is roundly rejected in the writings of Paul and there is no evidence for its support from the other Apostles. Thus, this could not be considered a denominational split because Paul implies that those teaching these things were not true believers, but rather teachers of a false religion based on salvation by works.

Certainly, it is human nature to label people and groups of people so we can easily categorize them and decide whether or not to trust them. But the only label the Lord Jesus spoke of in His prayer for unity was the label and mark that the Holy Spirit places on each believer. This is the mark that we need to be expecting to see in a claimed believer in Jesus. How will we know these that are the true Church? By their fruits – the fruit of the Holy Spirit.

In fact, this was what the Lord spoke to me regarding affiliating with the ministry in which I currently serve. When I was praying about joining Ellel Ministries as the director of the US operations, I had many voices of good and well-meaning people speaking into the decision. In a multitude of counselors there is wisdom. But in the end, with key decisions we must make regarding God's leading in our lives, we must hear from Him.

As I approached the time to make a commitment or decline the offer to take the role of National Director for the USA, I had a number of people question my decision because the ministry had struggled financially for several years. The logic was that if God was really in support of and working through the ministry I was joining, why would the ministry struggle so much financially? On one occasion, just before I was to make the final decision, I had a conversation with a person I believed to be a wise, Spirit-filled believer who heard from God. Speaking of Ellel Ministries, this individual raised questions about God's hand being on a ministry that struggled so much financially – not knowing that I was on the cusp of taking the position at that very ministry.

The next day, I had planned to go to Ellel Ministries to listen to testimonies of the people who had attended a week-long healing event. As I woke up that morning, I heard the words of Matthew 7:20 over and over in my mind – "By their fruits ye shall know them." That afternoon, when I found myself at the ministry listening to the testimonies of how God had deeply touched the participants with healing and restoration, after each testimony, I heard the words again in my heart: "By their fruits ye shall know them." I knew the Lord was commending the ministry to me regardless of what outward appearances and others' opinions might have been.

This is an important word for the Church today. Many signs and wonders are being sought in the Church. But the Scripture never tells us to pursue experiences. Jesus, Himself, said that the life of following Him would not be easy. It would involve eating His flesh and drinking His blood – participating in the fellowship of His suffering.

The true test of whether something is Kingdom fruit or is something else is whether we see the fruits of the Spirit manifested in the people who have been impacted by that organization's or individual's ministry. Is the character and nature of Jesus demonstrated in the healing itself and in the life of the one supposedly healed? After the bright lights of a meeting or the emotions of the moment have faded, does the individual bear fruit consistent with the Spirit? This is the real test of Kingdom fruitfulness.

I believe the Lord wants us to avoid being enamored with the wow factor and emotions of some of the supernatural things we witness in various meetings and look for the fruit of the Spirit in the lives of those who have supposedly been healed. Similarly, we should not simply partner with those who have a statement of beliefs that appears to be similar to or identical with what we believe.

We should only bind ourselves together with those who are demonstrating the fruit of the Spirit in their lives. This should be our guide to determine with whom we are seeking "unity in the Spirit through the bond of peace."

6

Breaking the Church's Identity

If the evidence we just examined points so convincingly to Jesus' plan for a unified Body, identifying themselves only as believers in Jesus and divided only by their geographic location, how has the Church found itself in a situation now, where a January 2014 estimate of distinct Christian denominations numbers them at 45,000?[4] And that number seems to be exponentially increasing annually, having numbered only 1,600 in the year 1900.[5]

The answer lies only a couple centuries after the birth of the Church. The original instruments of the founding of the Church had passed away. By this time, the fourth or fifth generation of believers was leading the Church. The very issues Paul warned the early Gentile church to avoid in the books of Romans, Ephesians, and Colossians – disrespecting various roles within the Church and forbidding the observance of celebrations of Christian faith on differing days or in different forms – had become a reality in the leadership of the Church.

Paul vehemently objected to Jews judging Gentiles for how they related to the Lord and trying to impose Jewish traditions on them. At the same time, he sternly warned Gentiles against thinking of themselves more highly than they ought and failing to remember from whom they received the Gospel, and to whom they owed a great debt of gratitude. But only a few decades after Paul's death, we see antisemitic tropes and vitriol infesting the language and writings of Church leaders. This was a foreshadowing of the significant breaking of the Church's root identity that was just over the horizon.

Respected Church fathers began publicly expressing antisemitic viewpoints as early as the mid second century. Justin Martyr (138AD to 161AD) penned these disturbing words in his Dialogue with Trypho regarding the Jews:

> We too, would observe your circumcision of the flesh, your Sabbath days, and in a word, all your festivals, if we were not aware of the reason why they were *imposed* upon you, namely, *because of your sins and the hardness of heart.* The custom of circumcising the flesh, handed down from Abraham, was given to you as a distinguishing mark, to set you off from other nations and from us Christians. The purpose of this was that *you and only you might suffer the afflictions that are now justly yours*; that only your land be desolated, and your cities ruined by fire, that the fruits of your land be eaten by strangers before your very eyes; that not one of you be permitted to enter your city of Jerusalem. Your circumcision of the flesh is the only mark by which you can certainly

be distinguished from other men...as I stated before it was *by reason of your sins and the sins of your fathers that, among other precepts, God imposed upon you the observance of the Sabbath as a mark.*[6]

We see in Justin Martyr's language not only his antisemitic views, but also a serious misunderstanding of the purposes of Shabbat – he saw it as a scourge and not a blessing. He seemingly had either forgotten or ignored Jesus' teaching that Shabbat was made to be a blessing for man and to identify them as being in covenant to the God of Abraham, Isaac, and Jacob – the Creator of the universe.

In a similar vein, Origen of Alexandria (185AD – 254AD) stated:

> We may thus assert in utter confidence that the Jews will not return to their earlier situation, for they have committed the most abominable of crimes, in forming this conspiracy against the Savior of the human race . . . hence the city where Jesus suffered was necessarily destroyed, the Jewish nation was driven from its country, *and another people was called by God to the blessed election.*[7]

These and similar teachings were the seeds of Replacement Theology and the basis for persecution of Jews by later generations of Christians. This may be one of the first documented teachings of Jews as "Christ killers" – an antisemitic trope used by many Christian and political leaders down through the ages since the time of Jesus as grounds for persecuting the Jews. Origen's statement that the Jews will not "return to their earlier situation" also flies in the face of hundreds, if not thousands, of verses of Old Testament prophetic Scripture referencing a regathering of Israel and a time when they would once again worship God as a nation. It also contradicts Paul's teaching in the book of Romans.

John Chrysostom (344-407AD), one of the "greatest" of Church fathers; known as "The Golden Mouthed," a missionary preacher famous for his oratory stated:

> The synagogue is worse than a brothel...it is the den of scoundrels and the *repair of wild beasts* . . . the temple of demons devoted to idolatrous cults . . . the refuge of brigands and debauchees, and the cavern of devils. It is a *criminal assembly of Jews* . . . a place of meeting for the *assassins of Christ* . . . a house worse than a drinking shop . . . a den of thieves, a house of ill fame, a dwelling of iniquity, the refuge of devils, a gulf and abyss of perdition. . . . I would *say the same things about their souls.* . . . As for me, *I hate the synagogue.* . . . *I hate the Jews for the same reason.*[8]

Church leaders like Justin Martyr and Origen laid the foundations for antisemitism to pervade Church doctrine and thinking so that by the mid fourth century, opinions like those expressed by Chrysostom were commonplace among Church leadership. By this time, the Roman Emperor Constantine had made Christianity legal in the Roman Empire and, in fact, supported it, although His motivations for doing so are questionable.

It was in this context that what has become known as the First Nicaean Council was called together at Nicaea. The top priority of the meeting was to discuss the nature of Jesus – was He of the same essence as the Father or was He a created being by the Father? This decision was not close. All but three of the bishops in attendance voted to affirm the creed that God the Son – Jesus – and God the Father were of the same essence.

However, an apparent side issue was taken up at the meeting that served to set the stage for the formal separation of the Christian Church from its Jewish roots. This decision at the Nicaean Council set the Church on a course for some serious antisemitic activity over the coming centuries. It is telling that this decision (and its outgrowth at later councils) was followed closely by the onset of what is known as the "Dark Ages" (between 476AD and 1000AD). In fact, healing and deliverance drop off precipitously in the same time frame as these decisions were made.

The issue was whether the celebration of the resurrection of Jesus should continue to be celebrated in conjunction with the Feast of Passover. At this time, the celebration of what we now call Easter (Jesus' resurrection) was still known in the church primarily by the term "The Pasch", because it was directly connected to the Old Testament mandated Feast of Pesach, or Passover, and Passover's follow-on celebration, the Feast of Unleavened Bread.

The council made the decision to separate the celebration of the resurrection from the celebration of Passover, Feast of Firstfruits, and Unleavened Bread. This decision was not based on any Biblical mandate or support. Nor was it based on the teaching or behavior of Jesus, the Apostles or any of His other disciples. None of them ceased celebrating the Levitical feasts. In fact, Jesus clearly participated in all the feasts and used them as opportunities to teach their Messianic meaning. The Apostle Paul referenced them in his teaching – he said of the Feast of Unleavened Bread: "let us keep the feast. . . ." More specifically, none of the believers in the early Church abandoned the celebration of Jesus' resurrection at the time of Passover. Rather, it appears the decision at the council was based solely on antisemitic views and attitudes of the Church leaders.

In a letter written regarding the results of the Nicaean Council the following statement is found:

> We also send you the good news of the settlement concerning **the holy pasch,** namely that in answer to your prayers this question also has been resolved. All the brethren in the East who have hitherto followed the Jewish practice will henceforth observe the custom of the Romans and of yourselves and of all of us who from ancient times have kept Easter together with you.[9]

This decision substituted a new method of determining when Jesus' resurrection would be celebrated and thereby dissociated it from the context of Passover that God had chosen for the time when Jesus would be sacrificed, and from the Feast of Firstfruits, the date He chose for His resurrection. This alienated Christians from the celebration of the Leviticus 23 festivals – God's Appointed Times – that had, until this point, been one of the Church's most significant worship celebrations with a clear connection to Christianity's roots in the Old Covenant and the Jewish people.

Thus, this decision by the Church fathers was a manifestation of the fruit of antisemitism which had invaded the Church over the centuries since its foundation, sown in by influential early Church leaders in the second century, like Justin Martyr and Origen of Alexandria. "The canon from Nicaea, pushed by Constantine, made it forbidden to 'celebrate with the Jews,' pointing to the undercurrent of anti-Jewish sentiment [seen] in earlier centuries."[10] Notably, it has been reported that although the entire first generation of Christians was Jewish, none of the 318 bishops who attended the First Nicaean Council had any known Jewish ancestry.

Epiphanius of Salamis wrote in the mid-4th century of the Nicaean Council:

> The festival of the resurrection was thenceforth

required to be celebrated everywhere on a Sunday, and never on the day of the Jewish Passover, but always after the fourteenth of Nisan, on the Sunday after the first vernal full moon. The *leading motive for this regulation was opposition to Judaism*, which had dishonored the Passover by the crucifixion of the Lord.[11]

Constantine wrote that:

> [I]t appeared an unworthy thing that in the celebration of this most holy festival we should follow the practice of the Jews, who have impiously defiled their hands with enormous sin, and are, therefore, deservedly afflicted with blindness of soul. ... Let us then have nothing in common with the detestable Jewish crowd; for we have received from our Saviour a different way.[12]

Theodoret recorded Constantine as saying:

> It was, in the first place, declared improper to follow the custom of the Jews in the celebration of this holy festival [*i.e.*, the resurrection of Jesus], because, their hands having been stained with crime, the minds of these wretched men are necessarily blinded. . . . Let us, then, have nothing in common with the Jews, who are our adversaries . . . avoiding all contact with the evil way . . . who, after having compassed the death of the Lord, being out of their minds, are guided not by sound reason, but by an unrestrained passion, wherever their innate madness carries them

> . . . a people so utterly depraved . . . . Therefore, this
> irregularity must be corrected, in order that we may
> no more have any thing in common with those par-
> ricides and the murderers of our Lord . . . no single
> point in common with the perjury of the Jews.[13]

These historical accounts make it painfully obvious that, if not before, certainly by the time of the council of bishops at Nicaea, antisemitic sentiment, and not Scriptural, historical, or theological concerns, was driving the decisions of Church leaders regarding festivals, celebrations, and observance of certain "replacement" holy days.

By contrast, we see Paul (the missionary to the Gentiles and the one that advocated for Gentiles being accepted as brothers in the faith alongside Jewish believers in Jesus) making every effort to observe the festivals. In Acts 20, we see the Gentile converts of Paul waiting until after the Feast of Unleavened Bread to continue their travels on Paul's third missionary journey. This behavior applied not just to the closely related Feast of Unleavened Bread. A few verses further on in Acts 20, we see that Paul was making a point of arriving in Jerusalem for the Feast of Pentecost, the Appointed Time of Leviticus 23 that follows 50 days after Passover.

It seems self-evident that the early Church was still celebrating the Biblical Feasts that were part of the heritage of the Old Covenant and helped identify the Church with the assembly that God established at Mt. Sinai. This makes consummate sense in light of Paul's explanation that Gentile believers in Yeshua are grafted into the Covenants and partake in their blessings (Rom. 11).

And God's Appointed Times are a blessing and inheritance because all of them speak of God's work of redemption through Jesus Christ. Each of the Appointed Times outlined in Leviticus 23 points to some aspect of Jesus' redemptive work. But Passover is chief among them in doing so.

It is self-evident that various forms of religion are characterized by their celebrations and holy days. The rejection of common holidays simply because they were observed by Jews, even though they were rooted in God's means and purposes for His covenant with mankind contained in what Christians call the Old Testament, necessarily served to separate the Church from its heritage and roots in the Old Covenant. Thus, division over the observance of these very practical physical activities that believers engaged in together to mark and highlight their worship to the Lord, must necessarily result in other divisions among believers.

Once the standard for the observance of holy days ceased to be rooted in Scriptural ordinances regarding the times for and kinds of celebrations, it became a matter of the tastes or desires of whoever happened to be the latest Church patriarch. Whatever the latest council or Church leader declared was to be a holy day or special religious celebration and however he determined it should be celebrated became part of Church practice regardless of whether any Biblical support existed.

Let us stop here and consider the issue of authority. Once the authority of the Scriptures and the traditions that had arisen around that authority over several millennia were abandoned, disunity was sure to follow. Unity can only come where there is clear authority. The less clear the lines of authority are in a given institution – whether it be a business organization, military context, school, or church – the more disunity, schism, and even anarchy will reign.

Had the Nicaean Council's antisemitic attitudes been a one-time anomaly, perhaps we could chalk up the rejection of a connection to God's Appointed Times outlined in Leviticus 23 as simply a hiccup in Church history. However, the truth is that antisemitic vitriol and actions to further separate the Church from the Old Covenant only increased at future Church councils.

As one Jewish author noted in a work published in the late 1800s, before the Council of Nicaea occurred:

> the Christians attended the synagogues [and] celebrated the Jewish holidays, [even though] contentions over the Passover were still on. A large faction in the churches of the Orient insisted upon celebrating the Passover at the same time as the Jews. It required the action of the Nicaean Council to free Christianity of this last and weak bond by which it had still been tied to its cradle. After the Synod all was over between the Church and the Temple, officially, and from the orthodox standpoint, at least; it required, however, the action of further councils to prevent the faithful from conforming to the old usage, and it was not until 341 A.D., when the Council of Antioch had excommunicated [Christians who observed the feasts] that unity of the celebration of the Easter was effected.[14]

After the Council at Nicaea and its follow-on councils at Antioch and Laodicea, the Church found itself wholly severed from its foundations and roots. Not only did Church leadership reject the observance of the appointed times, but they actually became hostile to any believer who continued to observe any of the feasts, and were particularly hostile to those still attempting to connect the celebration of the resurrection of the Jesus to the date of the celebration of Passover.

The definition of Judaizing was expanded in such a way as to be used to forbid the observance of the Biblical feasts altogether. At the Council of Antioch in 365 AD, the council decreed:

> If any bishop, presbyter or deacon will dare, after this decree, to celebrate Passover with the Jews, the council judges them to be *anathema* from the church. This council not only deposes them from ministry, but also any others who dare to communicate with them.[15]

Similarly, the Council at Laodicea decreed in Canon 29 that

> Christians must not judaize by resting on the Sabbath, but must work on that day, rather honoring the Lord's Day; and, if they can, resting then as Christians. But if any shall be found to be judaizers, let them be anathema from Christ."[16]

When these edicts are considered in the light of Paul's writings regarding celebrations and festivals, their anti-Biblical character is obvious. Paul clearly stated in Colossians 2:16: "Therefore do not let anyone judge you by what you eat or drink, or with regard to a religious festival, a New Moon celebration or a Sabbath day." Paul was encouraging the believers to not get wrapped up in legalism towards others in how the feasts and festivals of the Old Covenant were conducted, but to allow freedom and liberty and even creativity in how they were observed.

By contrast, the Church leaders during the 4th Century AD not only disconnected all celebrations, feasts, and festivals from the Old Covenant, but also made it a punishable offense to engage in celebrating those times on the Biblical calendar. Legalism had replaced liberty and man-invented celebrations and worship events replaced those ordained by God. Now the celebrations and festivals became subject to the whim of the latest Church leader. Is it any wonder that we now have 45,000 denominations within Christianity and no end in sight for the splintering of the Church into even more factions? How will we ever find unity among these widely varying traditions?

7

Healing and Core Identity

A good definition for healing is "restoring God's order" to a person's life. This simple but profound definition reflects significant truth.

When we are seeking to bring healing to a person, we must consider how the individual may have gone "out of order." The word "disease" derives from the idea that your body is not at ease. It is not functioning the way that it was designed to function. Thus, when praying for healing, we would do well to determine how a person is designed to function and seek the Lord on where the person has gone "out of order."

We are designed as body, soul, and spirit – three parts. Disorder in one part of our being will almost certainly affect the other two parts because we are one being. Our core identity lies in our human spirit. Although all three parts of us carry or manifest that identity, the place where our identity "resides" is in that eternal part of us that Scripture calls our spirit and implies exists from the moment of conception. God gives us our identity. It is not just a product of our environment or even of our human parents. Something of God is in every human being because God breathed into Adam and Eve the breath of life. Even if we are not born again, we have something of the life of God in us that separates us from the animals and makes us human. We are spirit and we have a soul and a body.

It is in this core part of us that God imbues our identity. From the time of our conception, the enemy is intent upon killing, stealing, and destroying us. If he can impact our core identity through emotional, physical, and spiritual abuse and wrong thinking, lies, and distortions, he can interfere with our ability to fulfill God's plans and purposes for our lives. Damage to a person's identity is the deepest "disease" that a human being can experience and hugely impacts all the other parts of a person's being.

Over the course of many years of prayer ministry with many believers who are experiencing various challenges and in need of all sorts of healing in their bodies, souls, and spirits, I have found none is more difficult and challenging to address than distortion and brokenness in someone's human spirit.

If, for instance, a person's sexual identity has been attacked through sexual abuse, they often begin to "feel" and behave out of a resulting false identity. Until they go with the Lord to the place of wounding and deal with the pain and hurt with Him, they will not be able to fully embrace their God-given identity. While memorizing Bible verses, or Biblically based songs, and engaging in positive self-talk may provide a measure of relief, only directly addressing the wound to the identity issues at the level of the human spirit under the anointing of the Holy Spirit will affect any real or lasting change. Only the Healer can touch deep-seated brokenness in a person's core identity.

I could share many examples of this principle and the extraordinary changes that we've witnessed in the lives of people when they experience healing in their core identity. For the sake of time and to preserve the confidentiality of those with whom I have ministered, let me simply share one personal testimony.

I grew up in a home with some very smart siblings and parents. Two of my brothers literally had genius level IQs. Because of sibling rivalry and other unhealthy competitive dynamics in our family (that stemmed from rejection), I experienced a lot of abuse related to my intelligence and was told many times I was stupid, especially by my oldest brother. Perhaps less severe but more painful was the disappointment I sometimes perceived in my parents' assessment of my intellectual capability – especially in my early years. I hadn't talked until I was nearly 18 months old, whereas my brother was talking at 9 months. When I finally spoke for the first time, however, I spoke in full sentences. I had some kind of learning disability that went undiagnosed back in early 70s. When they would test my IQ, it was competitive with my brother's. But I struggled with school.

This struggle with academics was exacerbated by being pulled out of second grade half-way through the year in order for our family to move to Indonesia, where my parents served as missionaries. Because of this, my schooling was interrupted several times. Reading even a basic primer was difficult for me until age 8 or 9. I developed a belief that I was stupid – that was my identity. These experiences had resulted in a belief that was reenforced frequently enough by those who were spiritually and emotionally close to me that I took it on as my identity.

Even after I received nearly straight A's in high school, I still identified as stupid or at least academically challenged. The idea that I might achieve anything academically was out of the question. When I went to Bible College, however, I realized that I was able to grasp the materials more quickly than most other students. When I decided to pursue my master's degree, I was shocked to finish at the top of my class. This success helped me believe that I could pursue a professional degree, and I applied for law school. Again,

I performed surprisingly well on the Law School Admissions Test and was accepted to four different law schools.

After the first semester of law school, I found myself ranked second in my class of approximately 160 students. By the end of that year, I was the only student in the top rankings of the class who had not received a tuition scholarship. I received a notice from the school that they had given me a half-tuition scholarship which they applied to my account for the remaining two years. They sent me a check to reimburse that amount for the year I'd just completed. I was surprised and overwhelmed.

I now had a lot of evidence that I wasn't so "dumb" after all. Yet, on the inside, I still felt stupid and doubted my ability to be successful. This affected my performance even at interviews for employment. When I landed a position at the top law firm in Missouri, I imagined that my success would be short-lived and was always waiting for the other shoe to drop.

Over time, however, my continued success (coupled with my rejection and false beliefs about my identity) spawned arrogance and condescension of others who weren't as "smart" as I thought I was. My behavior, rooted in rejection and a core identity of "being stupid," was still playing itself out in my life. Even after "making partner" – the brass ring for lawyers, especially in large top tier law firms like the one I was in – I still didn't feel, and in many ways did not behave, like I had the intelligence that God had blessed me with.

It wasn't until I began to deal with some of the rejection and distorted beliefs that were deeply rooted in my soul and spirit, and which were affecting my identity, that I could begin to embrace that identity without succumbing to pride and arrogance. I began to see it simply as how God made me. It isn't something of my doing. Conversely, I needn't be ashamed or feel inferior to others if I am not the smartest guy in the room.

When we can embrace ourselves in the identity God has given us, it not only gives us a lot of peace and helps us eliminate striving for approval, it also helps us carry a confidence that draws other people to the healing we have found in Jesus. It opens opportunities for us to share truth with people and to encourage people in their own walk, even when they might be "superior" in their capabilities or accomplishments. We can speak with boldness because we know who we are. Similarly, it avoids arrogance and allows us to minister to those who may not have been blessed with the same gifts, talents, abilities, or resources that we have. It also keeps us from envying those things in others and it destroys jealousy and wrongful competition.

The same is true for the Body of Christ. The Lord calls us His Body for a reason. Although we are many, we are one in the Spirit. As we deal with the competitiveness, jealousy, envy, condescension, and rejection that caused the breaking in the Church's root identity, and confess the sin of rejecting our identity in Israel and accepting a false identity that the enemy placed upon the Church, the Body of Christ will come into its true identity as the One New Man made of many people from two main groups – the nations (Gentiles) and the Jews (Israel). In this restoration of identity, we will experience and express a confidence, boldness, power, and authority that we have not experienced in the Church since the days of the Apostles.

8

Restoring the Church's Identity

As we mentioned in the last chapter, we must understand God's original template for a person before we can help bring that individual into healing. Similarly, if the Church is the Body of Christ, we must understand God's original template for it, and study how it has gone out of order so that we can help "restore Godly order" to it.

Since we are made up of body, soul, and spirit, disorder in any part of those three constituent parts of us will necessarily result in disorder of the whole. We cannot function well in our spirit when our body is in significant distress. By the same token, we cannot work at full capacity in our physical body when our spirit (our core being) or our soul (mind, will, and emotions) is out of order.

As we've seen in earlier chapters, there was significant breaking of Christ's Body (The Church) in the 4th Century AD when the Church was separated from her original identity. Just as I discovered in my own healing journey and in ministering to others, many issues people struggle with are healed when the person's God-ordained core identity is restored.

God gives us our identity. For example, our most basic identity is our gender – maleness and femaleness. This is revealed in the physical by the character of our sexual organs. But the core identity as male or female runs much deeper than the physical. It resides in the spirit of a person. When the inner core identity of a person is wounded or broken, the individual will seek to change the outer physical identity to reflect what they understand to be their identity on the inside.

Often when someone has been deeply rejected or a part of who they are has been deeply rejected, they react by changing their outward expression of themselves to wholly abandon that part of their identity.

In depth consideration of healing and the human spirit is beyond the scope of this book. However, the truths related to brokenness in the human spirit, as well as the process of restoring the human spirit, are applicable to our consideration related to restoring unity to the Body of Christ. Just as deep healing to an individual cannot come until that individual's true identity is restored, so healing (Godly order and unity) in the Body of Christ cannot come in its fullness until the core identity of the Church has been restored.

And the core identity of the Church is rooted in the Old Covenant. I am not talking here about being rooted in rabbinic Judaism. Rabbinic Judaism is as legalistic and has gone as far off course from God's intentions and heart for the Old Covenant as Christian legalism has gone off course from the heart of the New Covenant message of grace. Rather, I am talking about the Church's true identity being rooted in what we Christians call the Old Testament and Jews refer to as the Tanakh.

Ultimately, our identity is in Christ. However, Jesus was part of the Tanakh and was hidden in all of the practices and laws recorded there so that He could be revealed in God's perfect timing. Thus, to reject the Old Covenant is to reject Jesus' true identity. Jesus is the "root of the root." But Israel and the Old Covenant are referred to as the root stock in Paul's analogy of an olive tree in the book of Romans.

Moreover, Jesus said He did not come to destroy the law but to fulfill it. He fulfilled the law in His very essence. And He gave the Church His Spirit to help us abide by the law in our hearts. This did not mean an abandonment of the laws of morality as laid out in the Old Covenant. It was actually a raising of the bar from an outward behavioral morality, to an inward heart morality, so that the external moral behavior was a reflection of, and not a cover for, what was going on in the spirit. The outward behavior was simply a manifestation of a heart truly seeking to follow God's ways and bring glory to Him. Jesus' fulfillment of the law did not annul God's requirement that we live our lives in accordance with His moral standards for behavior in relationship to Him and to our fellow humans.

When we violate God's moral laws, we suffer the consequences in our bodies with all kinds of adverse physical, emotional, and spiritual effects. Our lives, and those of the people around us, are often destroyed when we refuse to follow God's ways in our lives.

Although celebrating God's Appointed Times outlined in Leviticus 23 is not a matter of sin (as is the violation of God's moral laws) doing so provides a practical means to worship the Lord for His redemption plan manifested in the person and work of Jesus and His Holy Spirit. As we will see in the next chapters, all these festivals or appointed times point to the One who would make a new covenant in His blood – Yeshua the Messiah.

These feasts *identified* those who observed them as adherents to the covenant relationship with the one true God. It was part of their *identity*. The loss of these elements of identity for the Church created a significant rift within the Body of Christ. Not only did it create division within the Church by essentially encouraging believers to create religious celebrations with no reference to any plumb line (other than the word of Church leaders), it also, in a very practical sense, removed the Church from its core identity in the Old Covenant. These decisions also separated the Body of Christ from the Feasts of the Lord – the very celebrations that represented Jesus and his Body – the Church.

When ministering to an individual regarding inner brokenness, it is often necessary to encourage a person to accept a part of themselves that they've long rejected. The Lord does not create people divided into pieces. Nor does He only accept portions of people while rejecting other parts. He doesn't embrace just the "good" and not the "bad" part of a person. This does not mean that He accepts our sin or is not offended by our sin. But it does mean that we can come to Him just as we are, and He will love every part of us – even that part that has been defiled or become unclean. He doesn't leave us in that state, of course. He wants to cleanse us and purify us and restore those areas that have been held captive by the enemy. But He loves and embraces the whole of our being.

In the healing ministry, we have found it difficult to bring complete healing to individuals who have rejected a part of themselves that they see as broken or defiled. They wear "masks" or pretend that part doesn't exist. In such cases, until the person accepts that defiled or broken part of themself as they really are and "brings" that part of themself to the Lord for healing, cleansing, and restoration, they will not experience complete healing.

To be clear, we do not lead them to accept the sin or defilement, but rather to accept the part of themself that has been bound in sin or defiled. If the person refuses to have anything to do with that part of themself, it seems that the will of the person is somehow excluding the Lord from coming into that place of need. The Lord will not override a person's free will and, if the person refuses to be associated with that part of themself, they certainly cannot bring that part to the Lord. This is sometimes referred to as dissociation.

Another key principle in healing, particularly regarding rejection, is helping people accept others as they really are. When an individual is wounded, they frequently not only reject that part of themself that they find objectionable, but they will reject others – and particularly those who have similar issues or problems. They reject that part of the other person that they feel is defiled or reminds them of their own weaknesses.

When dealing with past sin or wounding in such an individual, it is necessary to encourage them to accept that part of themself – *i.e.*, come into reality about what happened and what that did to them – and then to encourage them to repent and ask forgiveness for their own sin in the matter, forgive others for their wrongdoing, and turn away from the behavior or activity. They must completely renounce it.

We then ask the Lord to break all ungodly ties between the people, places, and things that were involved in the sin. We take authority over anything of the enemy that has attached to that place of wounding and defilement. Finally, we ask the Holy Spirit to bring the person back into Godly order in their body, soul, and spirit.

When we follow these steps with an individual and they are of a sincere heart, we see amazing restoration not only to their inner person and their way of thinking, but also to their external behavior and even their physical bodies. On the other hand, if an individual refuses to go back to that point and deal with the issues and part of themself from which they've dissociated, they will continue to struggle. They certainly cannot be brought into unity in body, soul, and spirit.

In the same way, in the context of the Body of Christ, where there has been sinful activity, rejection, and/or wounding in our collective past, we need to bring that part of our collective selves to the Lord and seek His healing. If we justify our behavior or simply ignore that part of The Body that was involved in sin and defilement (whether it is through our own choice or was placed on us by another) – if we dissociate ourselves as the Church from these unsightly past activities and/or refuse to rectify the misbehavior – we will continue to "act out" and we will remain in disunity. Spirits of division will be free to continue their work.

Thankfully, in the past two decades, we have witnessed an amazing movement in the Gentile Church to return to those places where these ungodly decisions were made and to repent of the antisemitism and ungodly behaviors that have fed the brokenness and disunity of the Church over the centuries.[17] But much more remains to be done. The broader Church has been largely oblivious to the problem and has thus made little progress toward dealing with these past sins. We must go back to the roots, both physically and spiritually, of the division and disunity of the Church. This is a work the Lord is doing in these days we are currently living, and He is calling His Church to join Him in the restoration process.

9

⧒⧓

Uprooting False Beliefs

As a boy growing up in Indonesia, I enjoyed gardening. I grew pumpkins, corn, radishes, tomatoes, potatoes, and even banana trees. The rich volcanic soil and abundant rain of Java, coupled with the high-quality seed I brought from the United States, made for some incredible produce. One thing I learned quickly about gardening was that weeds would choke out my crop if not dealt with. And simply chopping the weeds off to make the garden appear well kept would do little good for the health of the plants I was cultivating. The weeds had to be pulled at the roots so that the soil's nourishment could go to the vegetable plants or fruit trees I had planted.

In Florida, palmetto bushes are particularly annoying plants. They grow rapidly, they don't produce anything particularly helpful, and their roots run in long lines. When you try to uproot them, you wind up pulling up one plant's roots, only to find that it is attached to several more plants that pop up in other locations off the line of the runner root. To remove this plant from a garden is a major undertaking. But if unattended, these insidious plants will push out every other plant or shrub except very hardy trees.

A similar insidious plant in Florida and other tropical locations is the strangler fig described in the introduction to this book. Left unchecked, the strangler fig will kill the original tree and replace it with a banyan tree shell. The original tree and its identity are totally lost.

As we have seen in the previous chapters, by the fourth century AD, some serious weeds of antisemitism had not only invaded the Church but had taken serious root at the Nicaean Council to the point of pushing out some key identifying marks of the New Testament Church established first at Jerusalem. Like the strangler fig, a false identity was taking over. Like the palmetto bushes, the decisions regarding separation of the Church from its roots in the Old Covenant resulted in spiritual "weeds" taking over the Church. It certainly wasn't wrong to encourage creativity or even differences in the manner and calculations of the timing of observing God's Appointed Times. (In reality, various sects of Judaism at the time of Jesus disagreed on the calculation of the date for celebrating Shavuot. Jewish scholars still disagree about the timing of the years of Sh'mita (the 7-year cycle) and Jubilee (the 50-year cycle)). But the Church had moved to a position of forbidding believers from even recognizing the Appointed Times as set apart or in any way holy to the Lord. This was in direct contravention of Paul's teaching and the early Church's example.

The only way to deal with a bad root is to remove it. Jesus was clear that bad fruit cannot come from a good root, nor can good fruit come from a bad root. But each root will bear fruit after its own kind. Antisemitism, coupled with rejection of the authority of Scripture to inform the days that should be celebrations observed universally by the Church, are weeds that must be pulled up if the Church is ever to enter into full unity.

By saying this, I am not saying that special days and celebrations that are not part of God's Appointed Times outlined in Leviticus 23 cannot be part of our local regional or even denominational religious practices. But what I am suggesting is that the whole Church needs to repent of the antisemitism that motivated the Church's decision to reject God's Appointed Times as important times for unified worship to the Lord, and return to recognizing the importance of those holidays as special celebrations that coalesce the various strands of the Church around the person and redemptive work of Jesus the Messiah.

Just as Paul taught, we should not judge our brothers and sisters in the Lord regarding the means and methods of observing these feasts. But this is exactly what the Church did in the third and fourth centuries when it collectively anathematized believers who were attempting to align their celebrations with the Biblical feasts. This behavior requires repentance.

Some might argue: "I did not forbid the observance of the feasts and I certainly have no objection to people participating in them now. I didn't even exist, and I was not even a Christian at the time all these things happened that you have been discussing. So why should I repent of anything?"

But, as we have already discussed, generational iniquity for which no atonement has been applied, provides an open door for cursing to remain on our life and for the enemy to harass and otherwise affect us.

Thus, it is incumbent upon us as the Body of Christ to confess, repent, renounce, ask forgiveness for, and forgive, individually and collectively, in relation to the rejection and persecution of those who celebrated the feasts in the same manner as we dealt with antisemitism in our family line. As we've discovered, the rejection of the feasts by the Church was purely a matter of antisemitism and not based on Biblical truth or apostolic teaching.

In addition to being antisemitic, this decision rejected the core identity and identifying characteristics of the Church represented by God's Appointed Times. I believe this was offensive to the Lord, since they are, after all, His Appointed Times that represent His redemptive work and He asked those who worshiped Him to remember these special dates.

Why were these feasts so important to the Church that the enemy made it his mission to remove them from the Church's practices? In order to understand the meaning of their loss and how they are a key to healing, we must understand what they are and what they stand for.

But before we move to that topic, will you join me in this prayer:

> Lord Jesus, I bring before You this sin of antisemitism that resulted in the rejection of the celebration of Your Appointed Times simply because our forefathers wanted to distance themselves from the Jewish people. Please forgive us for our physical and spiritual forefather's sins and forgive me for any way I have participated in rejecting something You wanted us to enjoy. I forgive those in my spiritual and physical ancestry who misled the Church or continued in wrong attitudes and beliefs about Your Appointed Times. I want to follow Your ways, Lord, and celebrate the times and seasons You have appointed as set apart for You in the manner You would like me to. Please show me, Lord, what would be pleasing to You. Please also guard me against legalism or judgmentalism. I want to worship You and You only, God. In Jesus name I pray. Amen

The Lord's Festivals and the Church's Identity

A few months after the Lord spoke to me regarding Israel and the Jewish people in 2009, I was working my way through the Bible book by book in no particular order. I would read and study a book, placing no time constraints on the pace at which I worked through the Scriptures. I had purposed in 2005 to work my way through the Bible at a pace that would allow sufficient time for reflection as I went.

In the late summer of 2009, about six months after the revelation the Lord gave me in Blackpool, England, about Israel and the Jewish people, I finished the book of the Bible I had been reading, and as I asked the Lord which book I should read next, He clearly spoke in my spirit: "Leviticus."

If you polled 1000 dedicated Christians who read their Bible regularly and have healthy devotional lives, I doubt that, even among that relatively small group of believers, reading Leviticus would be at the top of their list. After all, what does the "irrelevant" book of Leviticus have to do with us Christians living in the twenty-first century? So I thought this was a bit strange, but I obeyed. I was going to have to read through it sooner or later.

A week or two into reading Leviticus, I found myself reading chapter 23. This is the chapter that outlines the Biblical feasts, or what are called God's Appointed Times or Festivals. Note that I am not calling them the Jewish feasts because the Lord did not call them that. Here is what Leviticus 23 says and what I read that day in early September 2009:

> The Lord said to Moses, "Speak to the Israelites and say to them: 'These are *my appointed festivals*, the *appointed festivals of the Lord*, which you are to proclaim as sacred assemblies. There are six days when you may work, but the seventh day is a day of sabbath rest, a day of sacred assembly. You are not to do any work; wherever you live, it is a sabbath to the Lord. These are *the Lord's appointed festivals*, the sacred assemblies you are to proclaim at their appointed times: The Lord's Passover begins at twilight on the fourteenth day of the first month. On the fifteenth day of that month *the Lord's Festival* of Unleavened Bread begins; for seven days you must eat bread made without yeast. On the first day hold a sacred assembly and do no regular work. For seven days present a food offering to the Lord. And on the seventh day hold a sacred assembly and do no regular work.'" The Lord said to Moses, "Speak to the Israelites and say to them: 'When you enter the land I am going to give you and you reap its harvest, bring to the priest a sheaf of the first grain you

harvest. He is to wave the sheaf before the Lord so it will be accepted on your behalf; the priest is to wave it on the day after the Sabbath. On the day you wave the sheaf, you must sacrifice as a burnt offering to the Lord a lamb a year old without defect, together with its grain offering of two-tenths of an ephah of the finest flour mixed with olive oil—a food offering presented to the Lord, a pleasing aroma—and its drink offering of a quarter of a hin of wine. You must not eat any bread, or roasted or new grain, until the very day you bring this offering to your God. ***This is to be a lasting ordinance for the generations to come, wherever you live.*** "'From the day after the Sabbath, the day you brought the sheaf of the wave offering, count off seven full weeks. Count off fifty days up to the day after the seventh Sabbath, and then present an offering of new grain to the Lord. From wherever you live, bring two loaves made of two-tenths of an ephah of the finest flour, baked with yeast, as a wave offering of firstfruits to the Lord. Present with this bread seven male lambs, each a year old and without defect, one young bull and two rams. They will be a burnt offering to the Lord, together with their grain offerings and drink offerings—a food offering, an aroma pleasing to the Lord. Then sacrifice one male goat for a sin offering and two lambs, each a year old, for a fellowship offering. The priest is to wave the two lambs before the Lord as a wave offering, together with the bread of the firstfruits. They are a sacred offering to the Lord for the priest. On that same day you are to proclaim a sacred assembly and do no regular work. ***This is to be a lasting*** *ordinance for the generations to come, wherever you live.* When you reap the harvest of your land, do not reap to the very edges of your field or gather the gleanings of your harvest. Leave them for the poor and for the foreigner residing among you. I am the Lord your God.'" The Lord said to Moses, "Say to the Israelites: 'On the first day of the seventh month you are to have a day of sabbath rest, a sacred assembly commemorated with trumpet blasts. Do no regular work, but present a food offering to the Lord.'" **The Lord said to Moses, "The tenth day of this seventh month is the Day of Atonement. Hold a sacred assembly and** *deny yourselves,* **and present a food offering to the Lord.** *Do not do any work on that day,* **because it is the Day of Atonement, when atonement is made for you before the Lord your God.** *Those who do not deny themselves* **on that day must be cut off from their people.** *I will destroy from among their people anyone who does any work on that day.* **You shall** *do no work at all.* **This is to be** *a lasting ordinance for the generations to come,* **wherever you live.** *It is a day of sabbath rest for you,* **and you must deny yourselves. From the evening of the ninth day of the month until the following evening you are to** *observe your sabbath."* The Lord said to Moses, "Say to the Israelites: 'On the fifteenth day of the seventh month the **Lord's Festival** of Tabernacles begins, and it lasts for seven days. The first day is a sacred assembly; do no regular work. For seven days present food offerings to the Lord, and on the eighth day hold a sacred assembly and present a food offering to the Lord. It is the closing special assembly; do no regular work. (These are *the Lord's appointed festivals*, which you are to proclaim as sacred assemblies for bringing food offerings to the Lord—the burnt offerings and grain offerings, sacrifices and drink offerings required for each day. These offerings are in addition to those for the Lord's Sabbaths and in addition to your gifts and whatever you have vowed and all the freewill offerings you give to the Lord.) So beginning with the fifteenth day of the seventh month, after you have gathered the crops of the land, *celebrate the festival to the Lord* for seven days; the first day is a day of sabbath rest, and the eighth day also is a day of sabbath rest. On the first day you are to take branches from luxuriant trees—from palms, willows and other leafy trees—and rejoice before the Lord your God for seven days. Celebrate this *as a festival to the Lord* for seven days each year. This is to be a lasting ordinance for the generations to come; celebrate it in the seventh month. Live in temporary shelters for seven days: All native-born Israelites are to live in such shelters so your descendants will know that I had the Israelites live in temporary shelters when I brought them out of Egypt. I am the Lord your God.'" So Moses announced to the Israelites *the appointed festivals of the Lord*. (NIV) (emphasis added)

I admit that I read the beginning of this passage with a relative lack of interest. But as I reached the middle of the chapter, the words of the passage regarding the Day of Atonement caught my attention. Specifically, I noted that the Lord emphasized three times that the day was to be a Sabbath rest day and three times

He decreed the Israelites were to "deny" themselves (which Biblical scholars agree means to fast).

When the Lord repeats something three times in the space of a couple verses, we need to pay attention. I thought to myself, "This Day of Atonement thing must be an important day in God's economy. Maybe I should find out when this happens on our calendar this year, take a Sabbath on that day, and spend time fasting and praying."

So I researched the date and discovered it was the day Jews call "Yom Kippur." This amused me because I remembered from my days as a practicing lawyer that my Jewish colleagues would always be unavailable on Yom Kippur. Even most of the more non-religious Jews observed this important day. We frequently had to schedule depositions and other discovery to avoid these holidays because there are so many attorneys who are Jewish. Tellingly, I had never associated "Yom Kippur" with "The Day of Atonement."

I had received teaching about The Day of Atonement and its significance relating to our redemption, the covering of our sins by the shed blood of the goat and the significance of the scapegoat. But never once had I related that teaching to the current celebration of Yom Kippur by my Jewish friends.

I use the word "tellingly" because the fruit of the separation of the Church from her Jewish roots and the Old Covenant had resulted in a rather large gap in my ability to relate the Old and New Covenants to one another. And even more importantly, it had served to remove any possibility that I would be able to relate my faith to the current practices of Jewish people so that I might, as Paul, in Romans chapter 11 implores, "provoke the Jews to jealousy."

Yom Kippur fell on Monday, September 28, of our Gregorian calendar in 2009. So I made plans to take the day off. Conveniently, September 28, 2009, was the Monday following our annual church missions' celebration, which I led. Thus, it served a dual purpose of recovery from ministry, and spending some much-needed relationship time with the Lord. I made plans to spend that day in our church's prayer room fasting, praying, and reading the Scriptures.

The day came and I entered the room sometime in the mid-morning. I prayed for myself and for my family. I prayed for my church and my country. I spent time repenting of any sins I could think of in my own life and that of my family, my church, and my country. I also spent time reading the Scriptures.

I simply prayed and read Scripture as I felt led. I don't recall exactly what I had read or what I was reading when something happened that I will never forget. Around 2 p.m., I was aware of the presence of the Lord in the room in a very unusual way. Time seemed to stand still. Suddenly, it was as if the Lord opened the top of my head and began to pour into my mind an understanding that each of the feasts of Leviticus 23 pointed to the Lord Jesus.

They all represented some part of His Divine redemptive plan for mankind. The feasts were either already fulfilled by Him during His first coming – as in the spring feasts – or they were to be fulfilled by Him as pictured by the fall feasts. I had never had any teaching, that I can recall, on this topic. I certainly had not been thinking about it or studying it. I had no input from the internet and no books on the subject – no outside influence that day whatsoever.

The three things the Lord profoundly impressed on me were: 1) These days were very important to the Lord; 2) They all pointed to and worshiped Jesus as Creator, Redeemer, and soon-coming King; 3) They were therefore important to the Church.

The most curious thing about this encounter with the Lord was that at the end of His revelation to me regarding how each of the feasts represented Him, I heard the Lord clearly say: ". . . and you will teach the Church about the feasts." My distinct impression was that I was not only to encourage believers to understand the feasts' Messianic and prophetic significance, but I was also to encourage them to memorialize them in some form or other in their own relationship with the Lord.

Let me stop here and explain a bit further so as to avoid any misunderstandings. I am not saying the Lord told me that I should encourage people to observe the Biblical feasts in the exact manner they are laid out in Leviticus 23 or in the way rabbinical tradition has directed adherents of Judaism to observe the feasts in the post-temple era. As a practical matter, it is literally impossible to observe or celebrate the feasts as they are described and ordered in Leviticus 23. First, there is no Levitical priesthood. Second, there is no tabernacle or temple to carry out sacrifices and other ceremonies. Third, Jesus' sacrificial death and shedding of His blood on the cross obviated animal blood sacrifice.

What I believe the Lord was saying that day was not a command to legalistically observe the feasts. Legalism is a deadly disease that will kill faith, love, and hope quicker than almost any other sin. Rather, the Lord was simply saying that He wants His Church to understand these important dates because doing so will serve a number of purposes in healing the rift between Jew and Gentile and bringing about His End Times plan for the One New Man. It will bring unity and focus to the Church on the prophetic events that are on the horizon of His divine timeline. He wants us to understand and celebrate the feasts because they will bring fullness to our faith and unity to our practice.

Because celebrating the feasts is an act of worship, when both believers in Yeshua who are bloodline descendants of Jacob (Jews) and spiritually grafted-in-by-faith descendants of Abraham (Gentile believers in Yeshua) celebrate the festivals of the Lord together, it draws us to the unity that Jesus prayed for in the Garden of Gethsemane.

I am certainly not advocating some legalistic observance of the Feasts of the Lord. I'm simply sharing that I believe the Lord is calling His Body back to its heritage in the Old Covenant that includes recognizing His Appointed Times. In the pages that follow, I hope you will see how the celebration of the feasts can bring a depth of intimacy with the Lord that many Christians are missing. I believe engagement with them will help bring all sorts of healing to the broader Body of Christ because it will promote and foster unity and unified times of worship.

Finally, the significant byproduct of the Church recognizing the importance of the feasts and engaging with them will be the provocation of the Jewish people to jealousy for their Messiah – a command that Paul gave us Gentiles in the New Testament (Rom. 11). Before we briefly consider the meaning of each feast, let's discuss some confusing terminology.

11

"God's Appointed Times" Not "The Jewish Feasts"

Read again Leviticus 23 as recorded in the last chapter. Notice God never once refers to "the Jewish Feasts" or "the Feasts of the Jews" or "the Jew's appointed times" or even "Israel's appointed times." Instead, in every instance, God refers to them as "my appointed festivals," "the appointed festivals of the Lord," "the Lord's appointed festivals," "the Lord's festival," "the festival of the Lord," and "a festival to the Lord." No less than nine times in Leviticus 23 does God refer to these special days as His festivals. They were never meant to belong exclusively to the Jews. They belong to God and anyone who claims to worship Him.

As if that wasn't enough emphasis, God finishes the chapter with "the appointed festivals of the Lord." Many people refer to these festivals as the "Jewish festivals" because they have been taught overtly, or by implication, that God somehow directed that they cease being remembered as special days in the New Testament. There is absolutely no evidence to support this proposition. In fact, the opposite is true. Jesus, the disciples, the Apostles, and even the Apostle Paul – the missionary to the Gentiles – continued to participate in the Festivals of the Lord.

Some point to passages in the book of Colossians in support of the proposition that the Lord has done away with any recognition or celebration of the feasts. As any good trial lawyer might object at trial, this "assumes facts not in evidence." There is no evidence Paul was saying that Christians should cease celebrating the feasts. He was simply saying that how and when certain festivals and days were observed should not became a point of contention because they are only a type and shadow of what should be central to all of them and that is Jesus Christ. Many of these disputes were arising because some Jewish believers were insisting that these practices were matters of sanctification and *required* for salvation, and they were nitpicking the manner in which certain festivals were being celebrated. The Apostles settled all these disputes when they wrote to the Gentile church:

> We have heard that some went out from us without our authorization and disturbed you, troubling your minds by what they said. So we all agreed to choose some men and send them to you with our dear friends Barnabas and Paul — men who have risked their lives for the name of our Lord Jesus Christ. Therefore we are sending Judas and Silas to confirm by word of mouth what we are writing. It seemed good to the Holy Spirit and to us not to burden you with anything beyond the following requirements: You are to abstain from food sacrificed to idols, from blood, from the meat of strangled animals and from

sexual immorality. You will do well to avoid these things. Acts 15:24-29 (NIV)

Moreover, God had said similar things to the Israelites through the Old Testament prophets. Just as Paul corrected the Colossians, so God rebuked the Israelites for losing the meaning and purpose of His Appointed Times. He told the Jewish people through the prophet Isaiah:

> New Moons, Sabbaths and convocations—I cannot bear your worthless assemblies. Your New Moon feasts and your appointed festivals I hate with all my being. They have become a burden to me; I am weary of bearing them. When you spread out your hands in prayer, I hide my eyes from you; even when you offer many prayers, I am not listening. (Isaiah 1:14-15) (NIV)

Even though God stated He hated their celebration of the feasts, He was not instructing them to cease remembering them. He just wanted them doing so with the right heart. They had lost the meaning of the appointed times and were celebrating them out of duty, obligation, and pride. This was the sort of error that Paul was dealing with among the Colossians. They had lost the point of the festivals. Paul was correcting this.

Still others argue that God's Appointed Times as outlined in Leviticus 23 have been fulfilled in Jesus. Therefore, it is no longer necessary or even appropriate to memorialize these special dates on the annual Church calendar.

First, this argument is surprising, considering that we still celebrate Easter, Christmas, Pentecost, and many other dates on the Christian calendar that represent Jesus' redemptive work. Second, even if the spring feasts have been "fulfilled" by Jesus when he was here 2000 years ago, the fall feasts have yet to be fulfilled and won't be until Jesus' Second Coming. Third, if Jesus' first coming has "fulfilled" the feasts such that they need not, and indeed must not, be celebrated, why does the prophet Zachariah declare that the Feast of Tabernacles will be celebrated by all nations during what most scholars believe is referring to the Millennial reign of Jesus, and nations who refuse to come up to Jerusalem for that celebration will receive no rain. This seems really odd if Jesus' "fulfilling" the meaning of the feasts makes them no longer relevant to God's people.

The significance of Moed

But perhaps the key reason the Church should be celebrating the feasts today comes from the Hebrew meaning for what is translated into English in Leviticus 23 as "appointed time." The word "moed" literally means "God-set appointment." It means an appointment to meet and fellowship with God. It can refer to both a set date and a set place. Moed also is used to refer to the set date for the time of the end and is used as the name of the New Jerusalem.

Strong's Exhaustive Concordance defines moed as follows:

> properly, an appointment, i.e. A fixed time or season; specifically, a festival; conventionally a year; by implication, an assembly (as convened for a definite purpose); technically the congregation; by extension, the place of meeting; also a signal (as appointed beforehand) -- appointed (sign, time), (place of, solemn) assembly, congregation, (set, solemn) feast, (appointed, due) season, solemn(-ity), synogogue, (set) time (appointed).[18]

Jewish commentators define it as

> [s]pecial days when [we] "meet," as it were, with God. Just as *Moed* in space refers to the locality which men have as their appointed place of assembly for an appointed purpose, so *Moed* in time is a point in time which summons us communally to an appointed activity – in this case an inner activity. Thus *Moadim* are the days which stand out from the other days of the year. They summon us from our everyday life to halt and to dedicate all our spiritual activity to them. From this point of view, Sabbath and Yom Kippur are also *Moadim*. The *Moadim* interrupt the ordinary activities of our life and give us the spirit, power and consecration for the future or they eradicate such evil consequences of past activity as are deadly to body and spirit and thus restore to us lost purity and the hope of blessing.[19]

Moed is first mentioned in the Bible in Genesis 1:14 during creation, when God said that the lights in the heavens should divide the day from the night and be for signs and seasons. The word "seasons" is rooted in the word *moed*. We see that God's creative order is tied to His order for us. As we come into order with His purposes for us, in the places He designates, at the times He sets, He will reveal His plans and purposes to us.

So we see that *moed* are not "the Jewish feasts" - although the Jews kept their celebration "alive" through the centuries and millennia - they are times that God appointed. He set them. Who are we to change or forget them?

Imagine for a moment that God called you on your mobile phone. You know it's God. He says your name and then states,

"Please meet Me at Starbucks at 8 a.m. next Tuesday morning." Or perhaps He simply refers to sunrise and says "meet Me at sunrise at Starbucks (in the closest town to you)." Who of us would ignore His request? I imagine most of us would spend the night at our nearest Starbucks to avoid any possibility of missing the appointment.

Let's take it a step further. We have the same scenario, only He writes you a letter. You absolutely know it is from God. God says in the letter that, on a particular date, He would like to meet with you. He has something to share with you that is very important. He doesn't designate a place, He simply asks you to set a particular time apart for Him to meet with you. He will come to you. In fact, you are part of an exclusive group He's calling together on that date, and He will meet with you and the group collectively that day. You are to set that day aside and wait for Him to arrive.

How many of us would ignore His request? How many of us would try to find a way to explain it away? If there was even a small chance that we were reading the plain language of His letter correctly – that we should set this day apart for Him to meet with us – wouldn't we do it? How many of us would say to someone we highly respected or who was due high honor, when they asked us to meet with them at a certain time and place, something like, "well, I know you said you wanted to meet with me, but that's not part of my traditions?" Can you imagine yourself telling your favorite US president, "I don't like the dates you offered. But I'll make time for you when I can. In fact, Mr. President, why don't you just show up on this date? I've made some space for you then."

Recall my experience when I read Leviticus 23 in the fall of 2009 and felt God wanted me to set The Day of Atonement apart to fast and pray. I didn't know all of this information about "appointed times" and *moed* and the deeper prophetic meaning of the feasts. I knew literally nothing. I hadn't studied any of it. I simply came to the appointment He asked me to make with Him and I had one of the most profound and life changing meetings with the Lord of my entire Christian life. I had a *moed* (an appointment) with God on one of His *moedim* (appointed days).

Let me share another similar story about a friend who, when I shared what the Lord had showed me about the feasts, seemed initially very skeptical. Although he loved Israel and understood God's purposes for restoring the Jewish people, he was not at all excited about the proposition that the Church should be recognizing the importance of the feasts referenced in Leviticus 23. Like many other Christians, he had encountered people who spoke about the feasts and who were very legalistic about them and condemning or judgmental about those who did not participate in or engage with the feasts. Even though he respected me and knew that I was not concocting a story about what I'd heard the Lord say, he was incredulous. Being Dutch, and quite direct, he was fairly dismissive of it.

A few years after I first shared with him about my understanding regarding the feasts and what I felt the Lord had said, he called me. It was the fall of that year (perhaps 4 years ago at the time of this writing). He shared excitedly what had happened just a day or two earlier.

One day, he was walking the property of the ministry where he served and was spending time with the Lord. During this walk and conversation with the Lord, my friend related that it was like an open heaven. The Lord was speaking to him so clearly about so many things. He was shocked by the clarity and content of what he was receiving from the Lord. So he stopped and asked the Lord why He was speaking so clearly. He wondered if someone was praying specifically for him that day. The answer came back from the Lord, "It is the Feast of Trumpets" and He told my friend to check the calendar. The Lord also told him to read I Thessalonians 4 – which is all about the Lord's second coming and relates to the prophetic meaning of the Feast of Trumpets (as we will see in detail in another chapter).

My friend described this as a "profound experience," after which he had no doubt that these times were important to the Lord and to believers. He'd had an appointment with the Lord "by accident" on one of the Lord's special Appointment Days.

This is really the heart of the feasts. The Lord wants us to meet with Him. He has designated certain days and times in the year for us to do that. Of course the Lord will hear the prayer of any of His children any time they come to Him in humility and sincerity of heart. But God set these special times that He invites His children to meet with Him. I have found that He often has something special to share with me on these days.

This is the point I want to bring home to the reader of this book. God is *inviting* us to His appointments. He is not demanding or commanding. He is *inviting*. As the days grow darker, He has "set a table" for us in "the presence of our enemies." He has specific times on His calendar where He wants to reveal His heart and His purpose for His people. Perhaps this is why He called them "feasts" or "festivals". They are times He plans to feed us spiritual food, even though we might be fasting, as He calls for on The Day of Atonement. The Body of Christ desperately needs these times with Him for renewal and refreshing, for recommissioning and re-empowerment. The question is, will we insist on seeking Him on our schedule or will we join Him on His?

12

The Feasts of the Lord and God as Creator

Perhaps one of the most significant reasons God wants His Appointed Times reestablished as part of the Church's practice just before His Second Coming relates to worshiping Him as Creator.

At no time in history has the world system seemed so hell-bent on separating humanity from its Creator and His creation. As cities increase and the world system seeks to create spaces that are not subject in any fashion to the natural world and its seasons and rhythms, humanity gets more and more separated from the creation and the Creator.

Consider that, for most of human history, most societies were largely agrarian. People had to feed and support themselves by connecting with the natural world. Good weather was essential to growing food. Society generally accepted that we are subject to the forces of nature which a higher power controls. Even if people did not have

89

a personal relationship with God through Jesus, and did not have the Holy Spirit guiding them, they had a "God-consciousness."

This is rapidly disappearing as we become more insulated from nature and more dependent on human systems for our livelihood and for our basic needs.

We also see an exponential increase in a rebellious attitude toward God as Creator. We see scientists and politicians pursuing all kinds of plans that are hostile to the concept that a Creator exists, let alone that we should follow His directions. The world system claims that they are simply trying to preserve the planet. But the roots of these efforts come from a view that there is no God or, if He does exist, He has no impact on, or right to direct, His Creation.

Decisions on the use of natural resources, space exploration, technological, medical, and scientific developments, all are moving at breakneck speed toward attempting to completely remove any thought that God exists or has a say in how the world functions or what elements of the natural world should and should not be manipulated by human beings. From genetic modification of seeds, animals, and even humans, to attempts to manipulate weather patterns, to restrictions on use of natural resources that God has given us to use, the world system is running headlong into rebellion and away from God and submission to Him.

The Scriptures tell us that in the End Times such calamitous events will occur that vast numbers of the human population of the earth will be eliminated. Shockingly, the prophecies state that even in light of this, and with the knowledge that God is bringing these things to pass because of human rebellion against Him, they shake their fists in the face of God and do not repent (Rev. 9:20). This attitude has been around since the fall of mankind, but in the last decade, I have witnessed it strengthen and infect nearly every area of society, including the Church.

God's Appointed Times are intimately connected to the creation and by participating in them on God's calendar, we are recognizing Him as Creator. As noted in the last chapter, the first mention of *moed* in the scriptures is found in Genesis 1:14 in reference to the creation story. It says that God set the moon, sun, and stars to mark His seasons and times. Not only do they set how His creation will function, they are to be used to determine when His set appointments will take place with mankind.

Shabbat carries a similar implication. When God completed His creation, He rested on the seventh day, and He sanctified it (set it apart) (Gen. 2:2). Note that the Jews did not designate it as a set apart day to Him. God Himself set it apart to Himself and later commanded any people who recognized Him as the Creator to set it apart. It is an appointed time of the Lord.

Additionally, as we will see in the more detailed explanation of the meaning of each feast in the coming chapters, they are all rooted in agricultural seasons of harvest. They are intimately connected to the Creator's supply and provision for His creation, and they all reflect God's redemptive plan for humanity.

So we see the intimate connection that the feasts have with the creation. When we recognize them, we are recognizing God as the Creator and His authority to set the times and seasons. When we take time with Him on the dates He sets as special appointments to meet with us, we can anticipate a powerful anointing and experience with Him.

Imagine if all believers are meeting on these dates that the Lord set for them to gather and worship Him, imagine the power of the Spirit that will be released. If the Church could unify around the feasts instead of setting their own individual special days of prayer, fasting, celebration, etc., imagine the impact a unified global Body of Believers could have against the kingdom of darkness. This, perhaps more than anything else, may be why satan is so intent upon blinding the Church to the importance of recognizing God's Appointed Times.

Finally, God set a *moed* for His Son, Jesus, to come to the earth the first time. The Greek Scriptures state it as "the fullness of time" in Galatians 4:4. A review of Strong's concordance reveals that the three words used in the Greek have the same collective meaning as the Hebrew word *moed* – meaning a specific moment in time appointed by God for that purpose. And God connected that specific time to developments in His creation. The three wise men read the stars (which God said in Genesis 1:14 would be a means of telling the *moed* - not just for the day-to-day rhythms of the earth - but for the times He would meet with His people) and they used them to determine the general time and place of Jesus' birth.

Similarly, God has set a *moed* for Jesus' Second Coming when He will bring the Kingdom of God in its fullness, and set up His throne in Jerusalem. As seen in the coming chapters on the fall feasts, they all speak and prophesy about the Second Coming of Jesus. They are a rehearsal for the events that will actually take place when Jesus returns. Their celebration is an act of faith in the promises that God has made to those who have trusted in Jesus as their Savior and Lord. Even though the day and hour of Jesus' return is known only to the Father, the signs of His return will be demonstrated in the creation and are directly connected to the *moed* of Leviticus 23. God, as Creator, and Sovereign over all Creation has chosen it to be so.

13

Messiah in the Feasts - Sabbath

After I began to study God's Appointed Times, I found there are many good books that explain the feasts and even provide some helpful suggestions on how we, as twenty-first century Christians, can celebrate them. Thus, my purpose here is not to provide an exhaustive study of the feasts. For purposes of our discussion on healing the One New Man, however, we must have a basic understanding of each of the eight appointed times in Leviticus 23 and how each represents Jesus' redemptive work.

The festivals the Lord outlines in Leviticus 23 are: 1) the weekly Sabbath (Shabbat), 2) the Passover (Pesach), 3) the Feast of Unleavened Bread (Chag Hamotzi), 4) the Feast of Firstfruits (Yom Habikkurim), 5) the Feast of Weeks (Shavuot or Pentecost), 6) the Feast of Trumpets (Yom Teruah or Rosh Hashanah), 7) the Day of Atonement (Yom Kippur), and 8) the Feast of Tabernacles (Sukkot).

Therefore, excluding Shabbat (a weekly observance), we have seven appointed times each year that the Lord directed His people to set apart to meet with Him. In this chapter, we will cover the weekly Shabbat. In order to understand the other Appointed Times in Leviticus 23, we must first understand the principle and meaning of Shabbat.

What is Shabbat?

Shabbat, known in English by the anglicized term, Sabbath, literally means "rest" and is a weekly celebration that occurs on the seventh day of the week. God refers to the days of the week and the months of the year by number. Although some months were called by their Babylonian titles, incorporated into Hebrew usage during the period when Israel was in exile in Babylon, and are therefore used at various points in the Hebrew Scriptures, when the Lord spoke to Moses in Leviticus 23 and other places, He referred only to the relevant number of the month. God had the same approach to the days of the week.

Such is the case with Shabbat. According to Leviticus 23, it was to be observed on the seventh day of each week. When I was a child, I always thought the word "Sabbath" was synonymous with Sunday. In fact, people in the church often would refer to Sunday as "Sabbath" and I heard more than one sermon about not doing regular work on "Sabbath" – meaning Sunday. Indeed, I still remember the days from my youth when most businesses were not open on Sunday. These practices were a reflection of the so-called "Sunday Laws" that were enacted in most states even before the United States became a nation.[20] And they had their roots in the Biblical commandment to keep the Sabbath Day holy. Sadly, these Sunday laws were sometimes even used against those who celebrated Sabbath on Saturday.[21] But the reality is, every reference in the Scripture to the weekly Sabbath is made in relation to the day we call Saturday – the seventh day of the week.

God's directive regarding celebrating Shabbat on the seventh day predates Leviticus 23, Moses, and the Patriarchs Abraham, Isaac, and Jacob. It was established as a special day by God at the time of creation when God completed all His work of creation in six days and rested on the seventh. Genesis 2:2-3 states:

> And on the seventh day God ended his work which he had made; and he rested on the seventh day from all his work which he had made. And **God blessed the seventh day, and sanctified it**: because that in it he had rested from all his work which God created and made. (KJV) (emphasis added)

Shabbat days happen on the seventh day of each week, but they are also part of each of the seven appointed times discussed in the following chapters. The Lord designated rest days during each of these times of remembrance and celebration. For this reason, in order to understand God's Appointed Times and one of the most relevant aspects of celebrating them, we must understand the principle of Shabbat.

The Purpose and Meaning of Shabbat

The purpose and meaning of Shabbat are clearly laid out in the Scriptures. Shabbat simply means "to cease, end, or rest." In most Jewish traditions, it is considered a precious gift and not a restrictive mandate. It is a time when families spend time together and reflect on God's blessings. It is a time to worship God for His care and blessing and our ability to work throughout the other six days of the week.

It is also an offering to the Lord of our time. The Lord teaches us that we should treat all that we own as belonging to Him. We are simply His stewards. Just as He proclaims that we should tithe from our financial increase, so too, the Lord asks for an offering of our time. Just as the tithe belongs to Him, He has asked that a specific day be dedicated to Him on a weekly basis. He asks us to observe one day a week when we cease from our own efforts and trust Him to provide for us. It is a reflection of our agreement with Him that our wellbeing and all that we have come from His hand, and we cannot take selfish pride in the blessings He has given us.

In the same vein, the Messianic meaning of Shabbat relates to the ultimate rest we will enjoy with the Lord when we will cease from all our physical work and go to be with Him. It highlights the truth that none of us can depend on our own righteous works to satisfy God's requirements. No matter how hard we may work to please God, "It is not by works of righteousness that we have done, but according to His mercy He saves us." (Titus 3:5) (KJV).

Taking Sabbath rest not only recognizes our total dependence on God for our earthly supply, but also speaks to our inability to save ourselves from ultimate destruction by our own works. The writer of the Book of Hebrews speaks of this in chapters 3 and 4 concluding:

> There remains, then, a Sabbath-rest for the people of God; for anyone who enters God's rest also rests from their works, just as God did from his. Let us, therefore, make every effort to enter that rest, so that no one will perish by following their example of disobedience. (Heb. 4:9-11) (NIV)

We enter into that spiritual rest through faith in the finished work of our High Priest, Jesus.

So observing Shabbat is actually not only beneficial to us

physically, emotionally, and spiritually, it also is an expression of faith that looks to the future of that Sabbath-rest the writer of Hebrews describes. We can rest in the finished work of Jesus Christ that works for our salvation. It isn't on us to save ourselves. That's good news, and worth celebrating!

So why does it seem that a seventh day Sabbath concept creates a negative response from many Christians? Most conservative theologians would agree that the principle of Sabbath is still a viable principle of a sanctified life. Few would oppose the idea that God has mandated regular times when we rest from our regular work.

And it's hard to argue with the extraordinary success of Chick-fil-A. This famous American fast food restaurant chain has observed every Sunday as a Shabbat since its inception. As one business magazine recently observed:

> Chick-fil-A is the most profitable fast-food franchise chain in the United States and the gap to number two (which just so happens to be McDonald's) is a cool million dollars per store every year. This is even more impressive when you consider the company's religious flavor, which means that every Chick-fil-A store closes on Sundays. So they're earning those incredible profits in six days while everyone else tries to catch up in seven.[22]

Here we see that even the secular media recognizes the phenomenon which doesn't make "business sense" – a fast food chain taking a day of rest and enjoying massively greater profitability per store than their nearest competitors who all work their employees 7 days a week. God's blessing on those who will honor a weekly Sabbath, especially as it relates to their work efforts, seems irrefutable – at least for a believer.

Objections to Sabbath

The objections or questions raised regarding Sabbath typically relate to two general areas: 1) must Sabbath be observed on a particular day of the week; and 2) what does it mean for us to "keep the Sabbath holy?" Let's consider each issue in turn.

Which Day?

Perhaps one of the reasons the Lord designated a particular day for Sabbath rest is that He knew our human nature would be such that if others were not observing rest, it would be hard for each of us to maintain our own time of rest. In other words, the principle of taking a day of rest can be followed without everyone doing it on the same day, but it is much more difficult, humanly speaking, for an individual to keep from violating the principle of rest on the day he observes Sabbath if everyone else continues working that day. Moreover, others will inadvertently draw the one on Sabbath off their Sabbath when everyone is observing different days of the week for their Sabbath. Perhaps this is the most practical reason the Lord picked a single day and directed mankind to set it apart as a rest and appointment day with Him.

The value of a unified Sabbath for all God's people was made so much clearer to me when I visited Israel. For the first time, I witnessed a society that actually put into practice the principle of collective rest as a society and culture. On Fridays at noon, stores, restaurants, transportation, and many other aspects of daily life began shutting down. The pace of life seemed to slow down each minute as we approached sunset on Friday evening – the start of Shabbat. During the day of Shabbat, we attended local Messianic services, but otherwise spent the day enjoying each other's company, resting, and eating. After all, we couldn't do anything else. Everything was closed, even if we had wanted to go somewhere and do something.

Like me, many Christians who have traveled to Israel to tour relate that the Sabbath is their favorite memory in Israel (provided they actually take a break that day). Everything slows down. There is time for reflection and relationship with God and family. It's a gift. Like an oasis in the busyness of life, it is a weekly place of peace that you can bank on to recover your own sanity and to enjoy time with others. It's a *moed* with God.

In the end, which day of the week the Creator God designated for this was His divine choice. As such, who are we to question it? This goes to the recognition of God as our Creator, who has the right to tell His creation when and how He wants to be worshiped. In fact, God made us in His image, and we are the pinnacle of His creation. When He completed His work, He took a day of rest and He also "sanctified" it, that is, He set it apart as a special time to remember Him.

This also goes to our identity. When we celebrate a day He has set apart, we are identifying ourselves with the Creator God. We are saying to the world that we recognize God as Creator, and we honor Him as such by doing what He instructed us – His created beings – to do in relation to the rest of His creation.

I am not advocating that we are sinning against the Lord if we do not rest on the day God designated as Shabbat. I believe the Lord has given us freedom to choose whether we will rest on the day He designated without our failure to do so being considered sin. Jesus made it clear that the heart of Shabbat is far more important than the day on which it is observed. He noted that the priests who worked on Shabbat took a different day for their Shabbat because they were required to work on Sabbath (*See* Matt. 12:5). He recognizes the practicalities that can interfere with celebrating Shabbat on the day He designated as Shabbat. Jesus also specifically mentioned helping our neighbor get his "ox out of the ditch" on Shabbat if that is necessary.

I am also not advocating people abandon their Sunday worship services. I believe you can worship on any day of the week and should be worshiping every day of the week on some level or another. What day we choose to observe a special rest day to the Lord seems to be left up to each person as a matter of their individual conscience as declared by Paul in Romans 14:5:

> One person considers one day more sacred than another; another considers every day alike. Each of them should be fully convinced in their own mind. (NIV)

The Lord certainly provides flexibility in practicing the timing of observing the weekly Shabbat. But it is not biblically correct to say that God changed the day of the weekly Shabbat or that God has erased the significance of the seventh-day Shabbat from His calendar. God has not changed the day on the weekly calendar when He rested after completing His creation and the day which He set apart for those who worship Him to have a weekly appointment with Him. To teach or imply otherwise is simply not supported by Scripture.

In practical terms, in my life, when I served as a pastor, I used Saturday for rest, personal worship, and reflection as I prepared for leading worship and otherwise ministering on Sundays. As the leader of a Christian healing ministry, I am frequently holding meetings or teaching on Friday evening and Saturday. Thus, like the priests of Jesus' day, I take Shabbat on another day – typically either Sunday or Monday. The most important aspect of Shabbat is the idea of coming away with the Lord and taking time with Him and with those He has given to us as biological and spiritual family. But when it is possible, I make it a point to set aside Saturday for rest, reflection, and renewal because it is the appointed time on the Lord's calendar that He set apart for us as a gift.

A final but important consideration relating to whether we should observe Shabbat on the seventh day, and which also impacts the observance of all the Appointed Times and their Shabbats, has to do with identification. The Appointed Times are an outward expression and identification with the Creator God and with the covenant God made with the Israelites. According to Paul, Gentile believers in Yeshua are grafted into the covenants and are participants in their blessings through our faith in the Root who is Jesus. Thus, celebrating certain days as Sabbath rest days identifies us with the Creator and with His covenant promises, whether it is the weekly Shabbat or the Shabbats set forth in relation to each of the Appointed Times.

For this reason, I advocate that, as much as it is within our power to do so, and without being legalistic, we should attempt to set apart the actual Shabbat weekly on Shabbat – the seventh day – for rest and time with the Lord. For, as already discussed, it was the very desire NOT to be *identified* with the Jewish people and the Old Covenant that caused the Church to break itself away from following the Jewish calendar for Pesach (Passover) in relation to observance of Jesus' resurrection.

In a perfect world, we would all take Shabbat on the seventh day. But I believe the Scriptures are clear that what day we choose to honor Shabbat is a matter of our own conscience. The principle of honoring a regular day of rest, however, is non-negotiable, and, if we choose to violate the principle of taking a regular Shabbat, we will suffer consequences in both spiritual, emotional, and physical breakdown and disorder.

What Can and Can't be Done on Shabbat?

Most Christians and Jews who care about the principle of

Shabbat, seem inordinately preoccupied with what activities can and cannot be performed on Shabbat. This originates in our fleshly response to the Lord telling us what and what not to do. Like Adam and Eve, since the first disobedience in the garden, we want to do what we want to do and we don't want anyone, including God, telling us what to do. So if we must obey, then we want to know exactly where the line is. Our flesh wants the letter of the law. God wants our heart and for us to follow the spirit of the law.

For example, it was not His heart to burden mankind or withhold something from us when He told Adam and Eve not to eat of the fruit of the tree of the knowledge of good and evil. Yet our flesh always wants to "bow up" against God's directives, rather than assume they are given for our best interests and blessing. If we would approach Shabbat as if the Lord is trying to bless us and not burden us or withhold something from us, we'd quickly capture the heart of Shabbat and it would be pretty easy to navigate – especially with the help of the Holy Spirit.

In Leviticus 23, the Lord directed the people to take Shabbat and do "no laborious work." Jewish scholars have long interpreted this language to simply mean you are not to treat the Sabbath day as a regular day like any other day on which you are working to make a living. In fact, they teach that doing "no laborious work" means simply avoiding work that will make you financially prosper or advance your ability to acquire financial gain or wealth. In this sense, it is a "sacrifice" because it costs something (by way of financial prosperity) to avoid the kind of work God is telling the people to rest from performing.[23]

This is the true heart of Shabbat, whether it be the weekly Shabbat or the special Shabbats that are part of God's Appointed Festivals. Our behavior in observing Shabbat recognizes the limitations of our human ability to provide for ourselves. Observing Shabbat recognizes God as our provider. We demonstrate faith in

Him that He will "take care of business" for us if we trust Him and honor Him by setting apart these special appointments with Him. In a sense, it is a sacrifice of our pursuing something we think will make us better off or richer, in order to trust Him with our supply.

This understanding makes it clear that God is not requiring us to sit like statues or worry about every physical activity we engage in on Shabbat. He also is not distinguishing between heavy physical labor and intellectual labor. For instance, a person who practices law for a living, might be resting in a manner consistent with God's intention even if he pilots a boat on Shabbat. While a person who is a commercial fisherman, might be honoring Shabbat by reading a recent US Supreme Court opinion on a topic in which he's interested. Pausing from writing this book to take Shabbat with the Lord takes a similar amount of faith for me as not driving a truck on Shabbat might take an over-the-road trucker. In each case, we must trust God to cover the potential "losses" we might incur by taking the time out with Him. It's all about our heart in trusting Him to take care of us.

He's simply asking us to come away with Him and trust that He will cover us, even if it appears that taking the time out with Him may cost us something. He is our supply, and He is the One that provides for us. We don't have to depend on ourselves. Of course, work should be a part of every able-bodied believer's life. God commanded "six days shalt thou labor" (Ex. 20:9). If someone does not work, he should not eat (II Thess. 3:10-13). But God also commanded rest one day a week. If God rested after six days of work, shouldn't we?

Jesus demonstrated that a legalistic observance of Shabbat is inconsistent with its ordained purposes. For this reason, He performed many healings on Shabbat. In doing so, He not only demonstrated the connection between healing and our bodies experiencing order that comes from resting in Him, He also undermined the pharisaical teachings that turned Shabbat into a burdensome effort at perfection that neglected to recognize the practical struggles of the ordinary person. Jesus taught that Sabbath was made for man not man for the Sabbath (Mark 2:27). In other words, we are not to be enslaved to the Sabbath. It was made for us as a blessing – not a burden.

We are free to do things that bring us pleasure and are relaxing to us – be that gardening, washing our car, or shopping. Certainly, we can do things that help others, even if it would otherwise be considered work. Jesus, Himself, used the example of helping others to refute legalistic arguments against His healing people on the Sabbath (*see* Luke 14:5).

But if we are treating every day the same, like an ordinary day of work, with no set apart time for God, where we are trying to generate income and take care of our livelihood, then we are violating the spirit of Shabbat. It is not to be treated as just another day. It is to be set apart. Shabbat was to be an act of faith in the Lord's provision and a physical demonstration of our acknowledgement of reliance on God for that provision. Thus, in our modern world, the question should be: are we doing anything on our designated Shabbat that constitutes an effort to sustain ourselves? Thankfully, we now have the Holy Spirit that helps us discern what is or is not activity that violates the spirit of God's purposes for sanctifying the Shabbat.

Many people who argue against a particular day being observed or argue against being restricted in any way on what they can and can't do on Shabbat, aren't observing the principle of a regular Shabbat on any day. It isn't about the day or even the details, it is about the heart attitude which is opposed to obeying God's mandate for man to take regular days of rest – setting aside a day that isn't treated as just another day of the week and honoring the Lord with our time on that day as well as relaxing and resting instead of running and striving. It demonstrates an attitude of ungodly independence from God and ungodly self-reliance and pride in our own abilities to provide for ourselves.

Thus, the principle of sacrificially releasing our plans and ambitions, and coming away for reflection, relaxation, and relationship with the Lord and our family are the principles that we should consider when determining what we should or should not do on Shabbat. How that plays out in each person's or congregation's lives is really between them and God. It is not a matter for us to judge or regulate. After all, if someone is skipping Shabbat, it's their loss.

14

Messiah in the Feasts - Passover

As was discussed earlier, Passover was the feast that was under discussion at the Nicaean Council. It is the first of the feasts in the Gregorian calendar year. It is also the first of the feasts on the Biblical calendar. As reflected in Leviticus 23, it actually happens on the 14th day of the month God designated as the first month, known as Aviv (or Abib) in the Torah and by its Babylonian name, Nisan. Passover actually predates God's directives in Leviticus 23, having been celebrated the first time in the year the Israelites left Egypt, and is the longest continuously observed feast, other than Shabbat, of any culture or religion in existence today.[24]

Passover was commanded by the Lord to be observed as a remembrance of when the death angel "passed over" the homes of the children of Israel as the final of the ten plagues was sent to take the firstborn son's life in every Egyptian household. The Lord had the Israelites kill the Pascal lamb that was without blemish and put the blood of the lamb on the doorposts and arch of the door. When the death angel saw the blood, he passed over that home.

Perhaps more than any other feast, Christians understand the meaning of Passover and its relationship to Jesus. Jesus observed a Passover meal (a precursor to the modern Jewish Seder) with His twelve disciples just before He went to His sacrificial death. He was the Passover lamb as Paul plainly states in I Corinthians 5:7.

What became known to Christians as The Lord's Supper or Communion was one portion of the Passover meal. During the course of that meal, the disciples eating with Jesus just before His crucifixion drank four separate glasses of wine and engaged in prayers of thanks and blessing before each. In modern Jewish Passover Seders, the third cup of wine is called the cup of redemption. When Jesus took this third cup, He stated: "This is my blood of the new covenant, which is poured out for many for the forgiveness of sins" (Matt. 26:28) (NIV). He then took a piece of unleavened bread, called Matzah in Hebrew, broke it and said: "Take eat; this is my body" (Matt. 26:26) (NIV). Thus began the Church's celebration of what Christians variously call "Communion," "the Eucharist," or "The Lord's Supper."

In the modern Jewish Passover Seder, traditionally held on the Eve of Passover on the evening of the fourteenth day of the first Biblical month, there are some amazing activities that the Jews engage in during the Seder that seem to be clearly types and shadows of the deeper Messianic meaning of Passover. At one point in the Seder meal, the leader picks up the "matzah tosh" or bag of matzah. This bag has three sections separated by pieces of cloth within the bag. So the bag contains three pieces of bread but in a single bag. He removes the middle piece of matzah and breaks it in half. He takes one half and returns it to the middle pocket of the matzah bag between the other two whole pieces of matzah. He then wraps the other half in a white linen napkin and hides it away. After more prayers and telling of the story of the Exodus, and following a formal dinner, the children are encouraged to look for the hidden piece of matzah that the leader had previously wrapped in a linen napkin and hidden away. Great rejoicing ensues when a child finds the hidden piece of matzah and brings it back from its hidden place to the leader in exchange for which he or she receives a gift. This piece of matzah from the linen napkin that had been hidden away is then used by the leader to lead the group in eating the matzah and drinking the third cup of wine – the cup of redemption. The connection to the body of Jesus being wrapped in a linen cloth, being buried or hidden, and then coming back out, resulting in gifts for the one who found it is clear to those who know Jesus.

The Feast of Passover is unmistakably symbolic of the redemptive work of Jesus in His death, burial, and resurrection. Not only does the modern Passover Seder clearly include elements that reveal the Messianic character of this appointed time, but the Lord and the New Testament writers also clearly link the two. When the Lord Himself celebrated the Lord's Supper in the context of the Passover Seder, it seems bizarre that Church leaders, only 300 years after His ascension, decided to forbid the celebration of the very feast during which the Lord had made these proclamations and birthed the sacrament of Communion that is held in such high esteem by all Christian denominations today.

Moreover, there is much symbolism regarding the new birth and life in Christ reflected in the celebration of Passover. The typical (non-messianic) Jew celebrates Passover simply as a time when God took their ancestors out of slavery in Egypt. The symbolism of deliverance from death and enslavement that is central in the traditional Jewish observance of Passover reflects the spiritual salvation we all experience when we pass from death to life at the time of our commitment to follow Jesus Christ as our Lord and Savior. We pass from Egypt (a symbol of the world) and the slavery it entails (enslavement to the world, the flesh, and the devil) and we are adopted as a royal priesthood and a holy nation (I Peter 2:9). Just as Israel was made a nation after coming out of Egypt through identification with the covenant given at Mount Sinai, those who put their faith and trust in Jesus identify with Jesus in the Covenant made in His blood (Matt. 26:28).

Passover, perhaps more than any other Appointed Time, lends itself most readily to Christian observance and to reconnecting Gentile believers to their roots in Israel and the Old Covenant, for it is the most obvious picture of the redemptive work of Jesus Christ connecting the Old Covenant and the New Covenant.

The Feast of Unleavened Bread

In Leviticus 23, Passover and the Feast of Unleavened Bread are listed as two separate events. In practice, Passover is the evening meal at the start of the Feast of Unleavened bread. Jewish people often refer collectively to both Passover and the Feast of Unleavened Bread as simply "Passover." They will refer to the first or third or seventh day of Passover.

Some people enjoy several Passover Seders during the week of the Feast of Unleavened bread. They may participate in a Seder with their immediate family and then join one or two or even several others, with their congregation or friends or extended family, on other nights of the Feast of Unleavened Bread. In I Corinthians 5:8, Paul exhorts "[t]herefore let us keep the Festival [speaking of the Feast of Unleavened Bread], not with the old bread leavened with malice and wickedness, but with the unleavened bread of sincerity and truth" (NIV). Paul clearly participated in the celebration of Passover and encouraged Gentile believers to do the same because he was speaking to the Corinthian believers, a predominantly Gentile audience, when he penned those words.

The key element of this feast is the absence of yeast or leaven from all foods consumed during the week it is celebrated. In fact, no yeast of any kind is permitted in the home during this week. Typically, the wife takes great care to clean the home thoroughly leading up to Passover (perhaps the origins of spring cleaning). By tradition, the father will be asked to go through the house looking for any remnant of yeast in the home just before nightfall on the Eve of Passover. A token crumb of bread is left in a pre-determined place for the father to find and ceremoniously dispose of before the sun goes down on the start of Passover. Religious Jewish families often engage the children in this symbolic search for any remaining yeast.

For followers of Jesus, this teaches some amazing truths in a very concrete way. Yeast symbolizes sin in the Bible. The Jewish tradition of cleaning the home of all yeast is an amazing picture of how it is incumbent on the parents, and particularly the fathers, to keep their homes free of sin and defilement. It teaches, in a very concrete way, the importance of keeping a pure home and regularly examining oneself for sin.

Abstaining from leaven over the course of the seven days of the Feast of Unleavened Bread symbolizes the desire for personal holiness. Passover represents the redemptive work of the Lord through His shed blood, while the Feast of Unleavened Bread emphasizes the importance of maintaining a separated lifestyle in recognition of that redemption and our priestly position in Christ.[25]

The discussion of the Feast of Unleavened Bread by the Apostle Paul in I Corinthians 5:7 and 8, referenced above, could easily be read as a New Testament command to celebrate the Feast of Unleavened Bread, and leaves us wondering how the Church leadership in the fourth century could have arrived at an opposite conclusion of actually forbidding the observance of the feasts, particularly Passover. Paul seems to be endorsing and even mandating its observance.

He is, at the very least, assuming it to be a normal part of the mostly Gentile Corinthians' spiritual lives.

Symbolically, Jesus is the unleavened bread. His body was the bread that was broken, and it was perfectly sinless, having no leaven whatsoever. He is the "bread of life" as John records Jesus saying. Interestingly, when you look at a piece of matzah, it is filled with small holes pierced through it for baking purposes, in rows, like stripes. It also has brown spots on the surface of the bread throughout from the baking process. Isaiah 53 records the Messianic prophecy regarding the Lord: "But he was wounded [pierced] for our transgressions, he was bruised for our iniquities, the chastisement of our peace was upon him and with his stripes, we are healed" (KJV).

We can further see the connection of the unleavened matzah bread that the Jews eat during Passover to the work that Jesus did on the cross, when we consider that Jews call the matzah at Passover "the bread of affliction." This is a reference to the bread memorializing when the Jewish people came out from under affliction and oppression of the Pharoah in Egypt.

By stating that the matzah of the Passover meal represented His body that would be broken for us, Jesus demonstrated that He became the bread of affliction for us so that He could bring us out of spiritual Egypt – out of slavery to sin and sickness and brokenness – and into a journey with Him to the Promised Land of our salvation. He took the suffering our sin deserved when He bore "our sins in His own body on the tree." (I Peter 2:24) (KJV). He became the "bread of affliction" for all of us – Jew and Gentile.

In light of all these connections, why would believers in and followers of Jesus not rush to celebrate Passover?

15

Messiah in the Feasts – Firstfruits

Just as Jesus died as the sacrificial lamb on the Eve of Passover, so Jesus rose from the dead on the Feast of Firstfruits. However, Jewish people today do not ordinarily observe the Feast of Firstfruits, unless they are very religious. It ceased being a significant event, mainly because of the destruction of the Temple. The ceremony of the Firstfruits involved the priest presenting a wave offering before the Lord in the Temple and sacrificing a year-old lamb. That was the extent of the activities related to Firstfruits. Thus, it apparently fell to rabbinical disinterest after destruction of the Temple in 70 AD.

Additionally, the date on which to observe Firstfruits was a point of contention between various sects of Judaism. The Sadducees and the Pharisees were split. Without explaining in detail, suffice it to say that the Pharisees and the majority of Jewish authorities at the time of Jesus' death believed that Firstfruits was to fall in such a way that it would have fallen on the Sunday following the crucifixion of Jesus the particular year of His death. Similarly, despite having a different method of determining the date to celebrate Firstfruits, which in any other year would have caused the date the Pharisees observed it to differ from when the Sadducees observed it, in the year Jesus died and rose again, the day of Firstfruits fell on the Sunday following Jesus' crucifixion. Thus, Jesus rose from the grave on the Feast of Firstfruits under either of the two differing views on how to calculate the date of the observance of Firstfruits because of the year that God chose for His resurrection![26]

The grain that was waved at the temple on the Feast of Firstfruits was barley. In the agrarian cycle in Israel, barley was the early harvest and wheat was the late harvest. Thus, the barley harvest always preceded the wheat harvest in Israel. So the barley harvest began in the first Biblical month, also known as Aviv (also pronounced Abib) or Nisan. The wheat harvest began in the summer months at the end of the barley harvest.

During the Feast of Firstfruits, the priests were to harvest the first sheaf of the barley crop in a ceremony which involved the priests carrying a sickle and basket to the predetermined location from which the first sheaf was to be cut. They would shout out four questions to the crowd that would follow them to the location to witness the cutting of the sheaf. The questions involved asking the people whether they should reap the harvest. In response to each question, the crowd would shout "yes!" The priests would then take the sheaf to the Temple and beat the stalks to harvest the grain and make flour from it. The "omer" of barley flour was the offering that would be "waved" before the Lord.[27] It was raised up over the head of the priest in the same way as Jesus was raised from the dead. It was the first fruits of the coming harvest.

Paul leaves no doubt as to the relationship between this festival and Jesus' fulfillment of the redemptive plan for mankind that it pictured. In I Corinthians 15:20-23 He writes:

> "But Christ has indeed been raised from the dead, the ***firstfruits*** of those who have fallen asleep. For since death came through a man, the resurrection of the dead comes also through a man. For as in Adam all die, so in Christ all will be made alive. Each in turn: Christ, the ***firstfruits***; then, when he comes, those who belong to him." (NIV) (emphasis added)

Once again, the obvious Messianic character of the feasts is not only apparent from general observation, but it is also clearly endorsed by Paul the Apostle to the Gentiles. So why wouldn't this Appointed Time be an important point of discussion and focus in the Church? These are amazing teaching tools, not only to prove Jesus is the Messiah, but also to illustrate, graphically and regularly through physical activities, the Gospel truths that Christians believe and relate them to the activities and worship practices of the Jewish people that have gone on for centuries.

It's sad that the Church cast aside the day the Lord set on the calendar He created, based on the cycles of His Creation, and which He required the Jews to observe for hundreds of years as a prophetic sign of what He would do to redeem mankind from sin, in favor of celebrating Jesus' resurrection on a random date totally unrelated to God's calendar, His covenants, or His prophetic words through the Old Testament prophets. This date was God's divinely chosen *moed* (appointment in time and space) for His resurrection. Indeed, it's not unreasonable to interpret Jesus' words "this do in remembrance of me," to refer not just to the taking of the bread and the wine, but to the whole set of appointed times that were all related and happened during the Feast of Unleavened Bread.

In any event, it's obvious that Firstfruits' Messianic meaning was realized in the resurrection of Jesus. He is the Firstfruits of many to be raised from the dead! That's good news worth celebrating!

16

Messiah in the Feasts - Pentecost

The Feast of Weeks, so named because it came seven weeks after Firstfruits, is more commonly known to Christians by the name Pentecost (except that the modern celebration of that date on the Christian calendar seldom lines up with the Biblical date of Pentecost). On the sixth day of Sivan, seven weeks plus one day after the Firstfruits barley harvest offering was waved before the Lord, the Israelites were directed to celebrate the Feast of Weeks or Shavuot (this was called Pentecost in the English New Testament). The Feast inherited its Anglicized Greek name from its occurrence on the fiftieth (7 x 7 + 1) day after the Feast of Firstfruits – *Pente-cost* meaning "fiftieth day."[28] In the year that Jesus died, both Firstfruits and Pentecost were celebrated on Sunday.[29]

In addition to being a celebration of the grain harvest, it was also a celebration of the giving of the law on stone tablets to Moses at Mt. Sinai during the Israelites' travel from Egypt to the Promised

Land. Jewish tradition (based on clear Biblical evidence) teaches that, based on the timing laid out in Genesis for the progression of the children of Israel from Egypt to Mt. Sinai, the giving of the law to Moses occurred exactly 50 days after the Israelites left Egypt following the very first Passover. By the time of Jesus, it was firmly entrenched as a dual celebration of the giving of the law and the start of the wheat harvest.

At the time of Jesus, Shavuot was observed with the following activities: 1) a Sabbath; 2) a holy convocation or gathering; 3) two loaves of leavened bread; 4) seven one-year-old male lambs sacrificed; 5) one bull sacrificed; 6) two rams sacrificed: 7) meal, drink and sin offerings made; 8) a peace or fellowship offering of two additional one-year-old lambs.

This festival also emphasized taking care of the poor and needy since the Lord had directed the people that during this harvest they were not to harvest all the way to the edges of their property. The book of Ruth is set during the Festival of Shavuot and reflects this command. We see in the story of Ruth that Boaz, in addition to having his servants leave grain unharvested at the edges of the field, directs his harvesters to leave additional grain on the ground for Ruth to retrieve.

Boaz, in the book of Ruth, is a picture of Jesus, since he is referred to as the kinsman redeemer. In the story, Boaz, a Jew with property rights in Bethlehem and therefore an inheritance in the land of Israel, marries Ruth, a Gentile. As such, it is a picture of the One New Man.

It is important to note that Boaz's compassion for Ruth and decision to care for her and even to marry her was based on her treatment of her Jewish mother-in-law, Naomi. In fact, Ruth famously replies, when Naomi tries to persuade Ruth to return to her own people and not continue with Naomi to Israel (and ultimately Bethlehem), "your people will be my people and your God, my God."

(Ruth 1:16) (NIV). Boaz ultimately marries Ruth and they produce a son, Obed, who becomes the ancestor of King David, who was the ancestor of Jesus.

Religious Jews traditionally read the book of Ruth during morning prayers on Shavuot. It is amazing that they do this while not understanding that their Messiah is pictured in the book by Boaz as the kinsmen redeemer or that it is a living example of the One New Man in Messiah.

Setting aside the Old Testament, including the book of Ruth for the moment, the relationship of Pentecost to Jesus and His redemptive work is obvious from the context of the New Testament Scriptures. For it was on this day that the Holy Spirit was poured out on the disciples. They spoke in tongues so that all those present could hear the Gospel in their own language. The Book of Acts describes the events:

> When the day of Pentecost came, they were all together in one place. Suddenly a sound like the blowing of a violent wind came from heaven and filled the whole house where they were sitting. They saw what seemed to be tongues of fire that separated and came to rest on each of them. All of them were filled with the Holy Spirit and began to speak in other tongues as the Spirit enabled them. Now there were staying in Jerusalem God-fearing Jews from every nation under heaven. When they heard this sound, a crowd came together in bewilderment, because each one heard their own language being spoken. Utterly amazed, they asked: "Aren't all these who are speaking Galileans? Then how is it that each of us hears them in our native language? Parthians, Medes and Elamites; residents of Mesopotamia, Judea and

Cappadocia, Pontus and Asia, Phrygia and Pamphylia, Egypt and the parts of Libya near Cyrene; visitors from Rome (both Jews and converts to Judaism); Cretans and Arabs—we hear them declaring the wonders of God in our own tongues!" Amazed and perplexed, they asked one another, "What does this mean?" (Acts 2:1-12) (NIV)

Because Shavuot was one of the three feasts during which all able-bodied men were commanded to go up to the temple to worship, and that time of year provided ideal weather conditions for travel, the city of Jerusalem was filled with pilgrims from the diaspora (those Jews living outside of Jerusalem and the surrounding areas). As is the case today, many of these Jews spoke another language as their native tongue.

This account clearly shows that the Lord planned this very important feast day to be the day on which He poured out His Spirit on the Jewish believers who had put their faith and trust in Him. They were now empowered and given boldness to preach the Gospel of Jesus to the ends of the earth. The Spirit of Jesus was given in a powerful way to His disciples so they could go into all the world and bring freedom and truth about the Redeemer and His Kingdom. Jesus chose the Feast of Weeks to do this redemptive work of releasing the promised Comforter – the Holy Spirit – the Spirit of Jesus.

It should not be surprising that He chose this feast to launch this part of His redemptive plan. Because it was the time when the Jews celebrated and remembered the giving of the Torah, it was the perfect time for Jesus to give us His Holy Spirit. Citing Jeremiah 31, the writer of Hebrews wrote of Jesus' fulfillment of that prophetic passage saying:

This is the covenant I will establish with the people
of Israel after that time, declares the Lord. I will
put my laws in their minds and write them on their
hearts. I will be their God, and they will be my
people. (Hebrews 8:10) (NIV)

The Holy Spirit has written the law of God on our hearts. If we walk in the Spirit, we will not fulfill the lusts of the flesh, even if we have never read the law. John 16:13 says His Spirit will guide us into all truth. The first Shavuot at Mt. Sinai was when God gave the written *law*, while the Shavuot immediately following Jesus' ascension involved the giving of the *lawyer*, our paraclete, who would not only intercede to God for us but would also interpret the law to us so that we could obey it from the heart. The Holy Spirit, as Divine Lawyer, advises us on how to keep God's law in our relationships with both God and man.

Finally, Pentecost is perhaps the most significant appointed time for the One New Man – at least other than the fall feast of Sukkot. We've already noted the book of Ruth's connection to Shavuot and that it is allegorically about the One New Man of redeemed Jew and Gentile. But there are several more evidences that Shavuot marks the inception of the One New Man Paul discussed in Ephesians 2.

Pentecost is also known as the Feast of the First Fruits. This is confusing because it is different from the Feast of Firstfruits. But Pentecost also represents the First Fruits offering of the wheat harvest.

In the activities of Shavuot at the time of Jesus, we see the two loaves of leavened bread waved before the Lord by the priest. These represent the Jew and Gentile. They are leavened, because they are not yet without sin, but they are Firstfruits offerings of the coming harvest of souls begun at Pentecost and continuing until the Second Coming of Jesus. They are two loaves, but one offering.

We also see two lambs that are sacrificed as a peace offering. These represent the peace that has come between the Jew and Gentile by Jesus death on the Cross (He died for Israel and He died for the nations) and the giving of His Holy Spirit that is poured out on all mankind, regardless of race. All those who put their faith in Jesus can now enter boldly before the throne of grace and seek help in our time of need. There is no middle wall of partition that allows the Jews to enter the Holy places but excludes the Gentiles in the outer courts. Through Jesus, the middle wall of separation has come down. Paul wrote to the Ephesians:

> For he is our peace, who made both one, and brake down the middle wall of partition, having abolished in his flesh the enmity, *even* the law of commandments *contained* in ordinances; that he might create in himself of the two one new man, *so* making peace; (Eph. 2:14-15) (ASV)

The book of Acts relates Peter's encounter with the Lord during which the Lord showed Peter, through a dream, a sheet full of unclean animals and told him to eat of them. After the Lord repeated this dream three times, the Lord told Peter to go with the men who would arrive to take him to the home of Cornelius – a Gentile. Peter obeyed. When he arrived, while he was still sharing about Jesus being the Messiah, the Spirit fell on Cornelius and all who were listening to Peter – Jew and Gentile – and they began to speak in tongues and glorify the Lord.

Thus, the outpouring of the Holy Spirit became the sign of a believer. And it demonstrated to the Apostles and all the Jewish believers that Jesus had come to bring salvation to the Jew and to the Gentile alike. This is the beauty of Shavuot as it relates to the One New Man. Without the Holy Spirit, unity between these two groups was impossible. There was a huge wall of religious tradition between them, including the mark of circumcision. But the Holy Spirit trumped all those concerns and tore down all the walls.

Again, we see how God's Appointed Times are clearly connected to His redemptive work on the earth. With our review of the Feast of Shavuot, we reach the end of those feasts that have been fulfilled in Messiah's first coming. We will next examine those appointed times that are yet to be fulfilled.

17

Messiah in the Feasts - Trumpets

Nearly every Christian scholar who studies or writes about God's Appointed Times divides them into two categories – the spring feasts and the fall feasts. They also universally recognize that, prophetically, the spring feasts have been fulfilled, while the fall feasts remain to be fulfilled.

Jewish people often call the three fall feasts the "High Holy Days." Similar to the spring feasts, they happen in rapid succession to one another starting with the Feast of Trumpets, or what has come to be celebrated as Rosh Hashanah – literally meaning "the head of the year." This is recognized as the civil New Year on the Hebrew calendar even though it falls on the first day of the seventh Biblical month. This tradition was most likely acquired from the Babylonians while the Jewish people were in exile in Babylon.

The Lord commanded a day of rest and a solemn assembly at

which the shofar (ram's horn trumpet) was to be sounded. This day signaled the beginning of what the Jews call the "Ten Days of Awe." It is so termed because on the tenth day following the Feast of Trumpets, the highest and most holy day of the entire Hebrew calendar occurs – The Day of Atonement – known in Hebrew as Yom Kippur. The High Holy Days transpire in the following timing and order:[30]

Day 1	Feast of Trumpets; Yom Teruah; Rosh Hashanah
Day 2-9	The Days of Awe
Day 10	The Day of Atonement; Yom Kippur
Day 15-21	The Feast of Tabernacles; Sukkot; includes Hoshana Rabbah on day 20
Day 22	The final day of Sukkot, also known to modern Jews as Shemini Atzeret; Day of Assembly; Simchat Torah

The Days of Awe are not a time for happy celebration, but are rather meant to be a time of serious reflection upon one's life. Jews believe that during this time God is reviewing each life to determine whether the individual deserves to have his name written in the Book of Life for the upcoming year. During the Days of Awe, Jewish people are encouraged to do good deeds or "mitzvot" to ensure their name will be written in the Book of Life for another year. Their rabbis teach them that there is no blood sacrifice now that the Temple is destroyed, and so doing good deeds substitutes for blood sacrifice. As we know, however, without the shedding of blood, there is no remission of sins. (Lev. 17:11; Heb. 9:22) And it is not by works of righteousness, but by His mercy that we are saved. (Titus 3:5)

The Lord commanded the blowing of trumpets on this day. According to Jewish teaching, the ram's horn is used because it was a ram that was caught in the thicket and became the substitutionary sacrifice for Abraham's son Isaac. The ram's horn may also have been adopted because rams take a leading role in the temple activities during the Day of Atonement – the appointed time that immediately follows the Feast of Trumpets. The ram's horn became a symbol of renewal and of rejoicing.[31] At some point, it also became acceptable to blow the Yemenite shofar (trumpet) that is made from the horn of a Kudu – a kind of antelope that is found in much of southern Africa.

Trumpets are also referenced in the Book of Isaiah as being used to call the people back to their homeland. Isaiah 27:12-13:

> In that day the Lord will thresh from the flowing Euphrates to the Wadi of Egypt, and you, Israel, will be gathered up one by one. And in that day a great trumpet will sound. Those who were perishing in Assyria and those who were exiled in Egypt will come and worship the Lord on the holy mountain in Jerusalem. (NIV)

Of course, the New Testament references trumpets as signaling the return of our Lord Jesus. I Thessalonians 4:16-18 states:

> For the Lord himself shall descend from heaven, with a shout, with the voice of the archangel, and with the trump of God: and the dead in Christ shall rise first; then we that are alive, that are left, shall together with them be caught up in the clouds, to meet the Lord in the air: and so shall we ever be with the Lord. Wherefore comfort one another with these words. (ASV)

The Hebrew name for the Feast of Trumpets is Yom Teruah. Yom means day. The word teruah means a mighty shout, either by a crowd or by a horn. This is the sort of sound that comes from a stadium of people or an army that is about to attack. It's the kind of noise we imagine that Gideon's 300 men released as they shouted, blew trumpets and broke clay pots, all of which threw the enemies of Israel into confusion. The passages from the Old and New Testaments quoted above make a direct connection to this festival and its prophetic significance as related to the return of Jesus.

The Jews also celebrate this date as their civil new year. They readily admit that it is not the Biblical new year, because the Lord said that the first month was the month in which Passover occurs, which is in the Spring of each year. The tradition of celebrating Yom Teruah as the New Year (Rosh Hashanah – literally meaning "head of the year") was acquired while the Jews were in exile in Babylon. Consider that the Feast of Trumpets now carries the dual meaning of the day when the trumpet sounds for the Second Coming of Messiah, but it also marks the beginning of a new year.

When Jesus returns, the Millennial reign of the Lord will begin. This will certainly be like a New Year celebration. It will be the end of an era of satan's reign on earth and the establishment of peace and justice under the reign of Jesus as King.

The Feast of Trumpet's connection to the timeline of Jesus' redemption of mankind is unmistakable. Once again, we see how the Feasts of the Lord directly reflect Jesus' amazing plan for redeeming the earth. And in these latter feasts, we can celebrate them expectantly, waiting for fulfillment, just as the faithful believers like Anna and Simeon waited expectantly for the Messianic fulfillment of the spring feasts.

18

Messiah in the Feasts – The Day of Atonement

As mentioned earlier, this appointed time is considered the holiest of the high holy days. In fact, it is actually erroneous to call this particular holy day a feast, which implies celebration and the consumption of food. For Yom Kippur is the only appointed time on which the Lord commands not only rest but also a one-day fast.

You may recall that it was on this holy day in 2009 that the Lord spoke to me regarding the feasts. I was fasting and in an attitude of prayer when the Lord revealed the Messianic character of His seven appointed times to me. In fact, the Lord repeats the admonition to fast and rest three times when referencing it in Leviticus 23. When the Lord repeats things three times in the Scripture, we need to take special note.

For instance, He repeated Peter's dream about unclean animals three times when teaching Peter that the Gentiles had been made clean through His atoning work on the Cross. The angels cry holy,

129

holy, holy, regarding the Lord in His throne room. Solomon repeats vanity, vanity, all is vanity in his writings in Ecclesiastes. The Lord asked Peter three times about his love for Him. So when we see the Lord repeat an instruction three times, we need to pay attention!

On the Day of Atonement, the High Priest was to make intercession for His own sins and those of the people. This was the only day of the year that he would enter the Holy of Holies in the Temple and the only day he would speak the name of God – YHVH – Jehovah.

After offering a sin offering for himself, the high priest would turn his attention to two goats that had been prepared for the occasion and which were identical and unblemished. By lot, he would determine which was to be killed and its blood used in the Temple and which would be the scapegoat. Both animals were used to make atonement for the sins of the nation of Israel as a whole. He would cut the throat of the goat chosen for sacrifice and would sprinkle its blood on the mercy seat above the Ark of the Covenant in the Holy of Holies. While this process of sacrifice was going on for both the sins of the high priest and then for the people, the scapegoat would stand waiting before the crowd.

The high priest would then place his hands on the head of the second goat – the scapegoat – and confess the sins of the people. A priest then took this goat to a wilderness location at the precipice of a high cliff. The scapegoat was forced over the edge to fall to its death.[32] Interestingly, the scapegoat would have a scarlet piece of cloth tied to its horn and, by tradition, if the scarlet thread turned white after the scapegoat was killed, the priests understood this to mean that the sacrifice had been accepted by the Lord and the sins of the people atoned for.[33] The priests and the people would rejoice upon receiving the news that the scarlet cloth had turned from red to white. As Isaiah 1:18 states:

Come now, and let us reason together, saith the Lord:
though your sins be as scarlet, they shall be as white
as snow; though they be red like crimson, they shall
be as wool. (KJV)

In the same manner as the scapegoat, the Lord Jesus stood before
the people while the priests laid hands on Him by hitting Him
and cursing Him with false accusations of sin. They falsely accused
Him and He died as the Scapegoat for the sins of the whole world.
Though He was perfect and sinless, as Isaiah says, on Him was laid
the iniquity of us all (Isaiah 53:6).

Interestingly, the Talmud records that 40 years before the destruction of the Temple in Jerusalem, the red cloth tied to the
scapegoat's horn, stopped turning white. The temple was destroyed
in 70 AD. Thus, the cloth on the scapegoat's horn stopped turning
white in 30 AD, the year most scholars believe Jesus died and rose
again.[34]

Just like the veil that was torn from top to bottom between the
Holy of Holies and the holy place at the moment of Jesus' death
(Matt. 27:51), this sign in the cloth that was tied to the horn of the
ram on The Day of Atonement in the fall feasts following Jesus'
ascension, attested that Jesus had been the perfect sacrifice and had
replaced the necessity of the sacrifice of animals to atone for sin.
This further confirmed that He was the Messiah that the prophets
had foretold. After Jesus died, the sacrifice of bulls and goats could
no longer effect the atonement of sin because Jesus had already laid
down His life once, for all time, for all mankind (Heb. 10:4-10).

Leviticus clearly states that without the shedding of blood there
is no covering of sin (Lev. 17:11). The sacrificial ordinances could not
permanently cover sin. Only the sacrifice of the One Perfect Man
could cover our sin once for all.

By placing our faith in Jesus and His atoning work on the Cross as the living, perfect sacrifice, we know our names are written in the Book of Life. On judgment day, the Lamb of God that takes away the sins of the world will come forth to claim those whose names are written in His Book of Life. All who are in Christ Jesus have this great hope. We will point to the shed blood of Jesus as our covering on that day.

The Day of Atonement was a day of national mourning and repentance. In fact, except for the sacrifice the high priest offered for himself so that he could be prepared to offer the sacrifice for the nation of Israel, sacrifices for individual sins were not offered on The Day of Atonement. The rams that were offered as the blood sacrifice and as the scapegoat were offered on behalf of the sins of the nation.

In Jewish tradition today, Yom Kippur is perhaps the highest holy day of the year. It is a time of fasting, mourning, and repentance. It is a day of coming before God and asking for His covering of Israel's national sins. But The Day of Atonement wasn't just about covering the sins of the Jewish people. It foreshadows the covering of the sins of the whole world when Israel and the nations repent of their rebellion against God and their antichrist worship during the time of the tribulation.

How can believers not recognize this significant day on the Lord's annual calendar? The Day of Atonement points to the day when Jesus will judge the nations for their sin and rebellion, and their mistreatment of Israel, and He will judge Israel for its rebellion against Him. The Scriptures record this time of mourning that The Day of Atonement foreshadows when the prophet writes:

> They (Israel) will look on me, the one they have pierced, and they will mourn for him as one mourns for an only child, and grieve bitterly for him as one grieves for a firstborn son. (Zech. 12:10) (NIV)

The Day of Atonement should be an incredibly important day for believers to gather, fast, pray, and prepare for Jesus' soon return, as well as for the nation and people of Israel to recognize Jesus as their Messiah.

19

❦

Messiah in the Feasts – Tabernacles

In contrast to the solemnness of the Day of Atonement, The Feast of Tabernacles or Sukkot is the most celebratory of all the Appointed Times. It is also known by the names of "The Feast of Booths" and "The Feast of Ingathering." By Jesus' time, it had gained such prominence that it was known simply as "The Feast."[35]

"Tabernacle" comes from the Latin word for "booth" or "tent" which is the meaning of the Hebrew word sukkah. Sukkot is the plural form of sukkah. The Feast of Booths or Tabernacles was so named because the Israelites were directed to erect temporary shelters for the eight days of Sukkot and they were to "dwell" in these temporary shelters. It was to be done in remembrance of their time of passing through the Wilderness on their way to the Promised Land when God was the Israelites' only shelter and supply.

Sukkot commences five days after Yom Kippur, giving everyone time to construct the shelter and be ready for the commencement of this final fall festival of the Biblical calendar year. It begins with a day of Sabbath rest.

The construction of the booth can be varied, and creativity is encouraged. By tradition, the only guidelines for the construction of these shelters are that 1) they should be temporary in nature; 2) they should have a roof made of natural products like palm fronds or branches. The idea behind this requirement relates to Sukkot being a celebration of God as Creator. The visibility of the sky and stars through the temporary roof of the sukkah is a reminder of God as Creator and our dependence on His provision. Many people decorate their sukkah with fruit because Sukkot is a harvest festival.

By tradition, people invite one another to come and enjoy a meal or just a time of fellowship in the sukkah. It is a joyful time for celebration with family and friends. In addition to the sukkah building process, the Scriptures encourage the participants to take palm fronds and willows and "rejoice before the Lord." Music and dancing are a must.

This feast is my personal favorite. I enjoy the significance and meaning of all the appointed times, and they each help create a beautiful mosaic of God's redemptive plan. But the Feast of Tabernacles brings a unique excitement and joy because it looks prophetically to a day when Jesus will rule and reign on the earth. There will be lasting peace, safety, justice, security, joy, and long life. In fact, for those that would argue that the appointed times are no longer relevant and should no longer be celebrated because Jesus is their fulfillment and He has already come, I point out Zechariah 14:16-19 which declares:

> Then the survivors from all the nations that have attacked Jerusalem will go up year after year to worship the King, the Lord Almighty, and to celebrate the Festival of Tabernacles. If any of the peoples of

the earth do not go up to Jerusalem to worship the King, the Lord Almighty, they will have no rain. If the Egyptian people do not go up and take part, they will have no rain. The Lord will bring on them the plague he inflicts on the nations that do not go up to celebrate the Festival of Tabernacles. This will be the punishment of Egypt and the punishment of all the nations that do not go up to celebrate the Festival of Tabernacles. (NIV)

This passage clearly refers to sometime in the future in a post-apocalyptic period when Jesus rules and reigns on the earth. Most conservative Bible scholars interpret this passage of Scripture as pointing to the Millennial reign of Jesus. So if the feasts should no longer be celebrated simply because we now understand their Messianic meaning, why will the nations be celebrating this feast during the Millennial reign of Jesus Himself on the earth?

For me personally, it is a joy to celebrate this appointed time. It was the first feast I attempted to celebrate in some fashion because it immediately followed The Day of Atonement on which I had received the revelation the Lord gave me about the feasts in the prayer room on Yom Kippur of 2009.

I decided I would construct a sukkah and do whatever Jewish people traditionally did during the week of Sukkot. I made the decision on the spur-of-the-moment, because Sukkot was to start just five days from the time I had received the download from the Lord about the feasts. I watched several YouTube videos and decided to follow one example of a sukkah constructed out of PVC pipe.

I learned a lot of lessons through the school of hard knocks that first Sukkot. Some were practical lessons about building a sukkah — don't try to build a sukkah from 3-inch PVC pipe. It's too heavy! I had to rebuild my sukkah three times and was forced to use a couple rolls of duct tape to hold it together!

But I also learned several spiritual lessons. One of the key things I learned was that physically doing some of these things brings the spiritual truth behind them into sharp focus in a way that merely intellectual reflection and study cannot.

For instance, as I was building that first sukkah, the Lord spoke to me about how He was my supply. I needed palm fronds for the roof of my sukkah. I had no palm trees in my yard even though I lived in Florida. The afternoon I finished my sukkah's frame and was ready to build its roof, my next-door neighbor cut his palm trees and left a pile of fronds by our front curb for trash pickup. The timing was perfect. The Lord supplied.

When I sat in the sukkah and had my daily personal time of prayer and reflection with the Lord, seeing the stars above me and nature around me, and understanding the meaning of Sukkot as related to God as Creator, I connected to God in a deeper and more meaningful way than I had before.

Sukkot also provided a natural way to share the truths about God with our children – God's provision and protection, and our need to be conscious of that truth and thankful to Him for them. I was able to share, with the "visual aid" of the sukkah, the story of God's provision for His people in the wilderness for forty years when they couldn't provide for or protect themselves. These activities naturally provoked curiosity in our kids.

We can, of course, experience and teach these sorts of things without celebrating the feasts, but the appointed times give us a regular opportunity (appointment with God) to refocus and reset our spiritual clocks. Sukkot provides a perfect time for us to reflect on all our blessings and to express thanks to the Lord for all He's done, as well as teach our children these truths in a concrete way.

I found that my young children really connected with this

particular God appointment, and they looked forward to celebrating it. We spent time as a family in the Sukkah each year during the eight days of Sukkot. We ate meals together and enjoyed sitting outside in nature during this time that the Lord had set aside for slowing down and spending time with Him and as a family.

A number of historians have speculated that the US holiday called Thanksgiving, that is now celebrated on the fourth Thursday in November each year, has its roots in the Biblical celebration of Sukkot. The Puritans were strong advocates of a literal interpretation of the Bible. Their spiritual leaders knew the Old Testament very well and it is more than likely that they were emulating this feast when they instituted an annual celebration of thanksgiving for God's provision that helped them survive a very tough first few years in the New World. This holiday was later proclaimed a US holiday by President George Washington in 1789.[36]

As we noted, Sukkot looks forward prophetically to the Millennial Kingdom when Jesus will rule the earth in the flesh as its King. As such, it is the time of the realization of the One New Man in Messiah – the Jewish people and the nations coming together as one redeemed people.

Sukkot foreshadows this truth even in the sacrifices that were required under the sacrificial system at the Tabernacle and later the Temple. In Numbers 29, God directed that 70 bulls be sacrificed over the course of the eight-day celebration of Sukkot. By Jewish tradition, 70 is the number of nations that came from the offspring of Noah. Thus, the priests saw Sukkot as a celebration not just for the Jews but for all the nations of the world. Today, because of this background, the Jewish people welcome non-Jews to celebrate Sukkot with them.

Before we finish our discussion about the Feast of Tabernacles, I want to clear up a confusing element of our Christian celebration of Easter. As part of Sukkot, Leviticus teaches that the celebrants are to gather palm fronds, among other natural tree limbs and plants, and "celebrate before the Lord." In Israel, during the time of Sukkot each year, the Jewish people carry what is called the Lulav which includes a palm frond, and they are to celebrate regularly with the frond by waving it and saying certain prayers during the week of Sukkot.

On the seventh day of Sukkot, however, there is a special celebration called Hoshana Rabbah. Roughly translated, this means the great hosanna or literally, "great save." On this day of Sukkot, religious Jews gather in their synagogues (or at the Western Wall in Jerusalem) and they say many prayers and sing various songs with increased joy and dancing as they proceed. They wave the palm fronds and they shout "Hoshana, Hoshana." How did this activity wind up being incorporated into our Easter celebrations as Palm Sunday?

Once again, we see the result of disconnecting the Church from its inheritance in the Feasts. Because the Jews recognize Sukkot as a celebration of the arrival of the Messiah to rule as King, when they believed that Jesus was the Messiah, they pulled this activity from Sukkot and were engaging in it when Jesus entered Jerusalem in what we Christians now call "the triumphal entry." The problem was, the Jews didn't understand the full meaning of their spring feasts and that those feasts must first be prophetically fulfilled before the prophetic meaning of fall feast of Sukkot could be fulfilled. They probably didn't expect Messiah to fulfill the spring feasts or the fall feasts on the very days that they celebrated them. But that is exactly what Jesus did during the spring feasts in His final year on earth. He fulfilled them to the day.

The Jews were looking for the conquering King. But they were in the wrong season. Jesus first had to come to earth and die as the suffering servant. Thus, the celebration of the palm frond has been mixed into the celebration of the resurrection by Christians.

Ironically, this confusion was caused because the Jewish people didn't understand the prophetic meaning and implications of the feasts as they related to Messiah. Perhaps this is a point of consideration for us Christians. Shouldn't we understand the full Messianic implications of God's Appointed Times, particularly since we seem to be entering the last of the last days when the fall feasts become extremely relevant because they relate to His second coming?

We see, then, that Sukkot pictures the ultimate fruition of the redemptive work of the Lord Jesus – to bring reconciliation and fellowship back to the relationship between God and man. During the Millennial reign, God will once again tabernacle with man. Through His Appointed Times, God has provided an amazing picture of, and roadmap for, His plan to redeem the world. Each feast, in its own unique way, signals the process and result of Jesus' wonderful plan of redemption!

20

Challenges to Healing the One New Man

Now that we have examined the Messianic character of God's Appointed Times, let's consider how and why we should celebrate them. As I mentioned earlier, the Lord instructed me to teach the church about the feasts referenced in Leviticus 23 after He showed me how each appointed time was connected to God's outworking of man's redemption through Jesus.

As I have reflected on exactly what the Lord spoke to me in the prayer room on The Day of Atonement in 2009, I note that He did not say "teach the church *to observe* the feasts." Rather, He said "teach the Church *about* the feasts."

In the course of processing what the Lord said and returning to it many times in prayer over the last 15 years (as of the time of this writing) since the Lord spoke it to me, I have become convinced that God did not say "teach them to observe the feasts," because He does not want us focused on exactly *how* to properly celebrate the feasts. If He had used the word "observe" I would have been caught up in trying to determine exactly the things I needed to *do* to properly "observe" them. This sort of thinking always leads to legalism.

God cares a lot more about our attitude and heart in celebrating the feasts than He does about exactly how we do it. God wants our motivation for engaging with the feasts to be love of Him and a desire to please and serve Him. He doesn't want us to participate in them because of obligation, fear, or to please men. He seeks worship that is in spirit and in truth. This is what He wants to motivate our decision as to whether and how to celebrate His Appointed Times.

The Lord wants us to come to these appointments with Him because we want to, not because He's forcing us to do so. He had to make strict requirements for the Israelites to celebrate them so that they would be clearly memorialized in the Old Covenant and their meaning and prophetic significance would not be lost over time. This was the assignment of the Jews, to carry these truths, as they did the Torah, so that the whole world could come to know the Messiah who is the fulfillment of all the law and the prophets and the feasts. The symbols and processes needed to be carefully preserved so that they would clearly prove to the nations that these truths the Jewish people carried were from the one true and living God. They were the identifying mark of the true worshipers of Creator God.

The Lord has a different agenda for His people in this season. I believe His current agenda is to use the feasts to bring the Church back to its true identity in Israel, to unify the Church, and to provoke the Jewish people to jealousy through the Church's Spirit-filled celebration of them. When the Jews see the joy with which we celebrate these appointed times they will be drawn to the One we are worshiping.

They are also a prophetic timeline and we are rapidly nearing the return of Jesus. They are an identifying mark for those who worship the Creator. Finally, they are to be the point of unified worship between Jewish and Gentile believers.

So the Lord is presenting us with an invitation. He is not mandating that we do it. Like many other principles in the Bible, He teaches us His ways and then leaves it to us to decide. In this instance, I do not believe He is saying that the Church is "sinning" if they refuse to engage with the feasts or if they don't celebrate them in exactly a certain way. This is why He told me to teach the Church "about the feasts." It is an invitation and a free choice, not a matter of right and wrong.

In a real sense, I believe the Lord is inviting the Church back again to His "family table." Even though we have separated ourselves from our Jewish identity, and, for that matter, from Jesus' Jewish identity because of antisemitism, He is calling us back. He's doing this because He is preparing to return soon and, as Romans 11 predicts, He will be sweeping many of His kinsmen into the Kingdom as the veil over their spiritual eyes begins to fall away and they begin to accept Jesus as their Messiah.

Jesus does not want His Jewish family to abandon His Appointed Times in order to "become Christian." Rather, He wants them to worship and celebrate them with an understanding of their deeper Messianic meaning and significance. And He wants the Gentile Church to return to their identity in the Old Covenant and in Israel so that we can be united as one big family of God.

This is an invitation, not a mandate. It's very much like He is inviting us to a family dinner party. He only wants us to attend the party if we want to. He won't force us to join Him.

Avoiding Legalism

As I began to study the feasts, I quickly came to realize that there are many groups and individuals who are talking about the feasts. There seems to be a significantly increased interest in the topic in just the last 20 years, and the level of interest seems to be escalating. This helped confirm to me that what I'd heard on The Day of Atonement in 2009 was a move of the Spirit and not just my imagination or some unique word the Lord had given to me.

But at the same time, I began to run across books and individuals who seemed to be taking the renewal of interest in the Old Covenant Jewish roots to a troubling place. They were advocating that dietary laws and other directives – things Paul seems to say in a number of his writings are issues of conscience – must be strictly followed. The implication was that failure to do so affects our sanctification. Simply put, they seemed to advocate that failure to do these things is sin.

They advocated observance of the feasts for similar reasons. Most of the authors or teachers who took these positions regarding the dietary laws and/or the feasts, claimed they weren't advocating eternal salvation by these works, but they were advocating either openly or by implication that failure to observe the feasts or keep dietary laws would affect a believer's holiness or "cleanness", *i.e.*, sanctification before God.

This alarmed me. I sensed that this was not of the Lord, but something of the enemy trying to inhibit the Church's openness to the feasts. What better way to raise a barrier to the Church engaging with the feasts than to create a movement that condemns and gets legalistic about them?

I have since seen the fruit of teaching that advocates dietary observances, and holiday celebrations as "sin issues." In fact, I personally observed some people who were running a good race in the Lord, as Paul talks about in Galatians, being "cut in on" (*see* Galatians 5:7 (NIV)) by these teachings which I believe fit the definition of legalism. In one particular time of discouragement about this, a Messianic Jewish friend of mine shared with me that he believed that this sort of legalism has an antichrist spirit behind it and will ultimately lead people to question the Messianic character and deity of Jesus. I have found this to be true. I've known of several Messianic believers, and even whole congregations, who have found themselves denying Jesus is God in direct opposition to the clear explanation of Jesus' deity in John Chapter 1.

In saying all this, I believe it is the right of any believer to abstain from eating pork or follow other dietary restrictions as the Lord leads them. These are "personal convictions" regarding which individuals have freedom. These are matters about which the Apostle Paul says, "let each person be fully convinced in his heart" – just like some Christians abstain from drinking alcohol or avoid watching movies of a certain rating.

So let me reiterate here that I am not advocating celebrating the feasts because we must do so to achieve righteousness or holiness or because failure to do so will defile us. What I am advocating is that the Lord is calling the Church back to some form of engaging with the feasts because these Appointed Times speak of Jesus, and anti-semitism is the sole reason the Church ceased to engage with them. This antisemitism caused the Church leaders to seek separation of any identity with Jews. This decision was rooted in jealousy and racism, not Scripture or sound theology. This is a poor reason to reject celebrations that clearly point to Messiah and the celebration of which are a form of worship to Him.

Moreover, I am not arguing for any specific legalistic observance of the feasts. Just as we should never rely on church attendance to save us or, in and of itself, to make us holier, I do not claim that observance of the feasts makes us holier. However, just like attending regular church services helps us focus on the Lord, encourages us to walk faithfully, and clarifies what should be important to us, so the feasts serve a similar function.

By the same token, just as the ways and traditions that churches follow in carrying out worship to the Lord on Sunday is varied and unique, so too the celebration of the feasts can be varied and unique. We do not have to follow rabbinical Judaism's approach to celebrating the feasts. Certainly, we would do well to learn from those who have been celebrating the feasts all along, namely the Jews, but we must measure everything against what the original Biblical guidelines are. We don't need to add to or subtract from those guidelines. Moreover, we need to follow the Spirit of the celebration more than we do the letter of the law.

As I mentioned before, the feasts *cannot* be observed with all the elements laid out in Leviticus 23 because animal sacrifice is no longer appropriate under the New Covenant and, even if it were, there is no priesthood or temple in which to carry it out. That alone removes a lot of the letter of the law regarding the practice of the feasts.

I suggest pastors and leaders thoroughly study and understand the meaning behind the feasts as we have discussed in the last several chapters and then set aside the appointed times to celebrate them in a manner consistent with the heart and meaning of the feasts, keeping in mind that physical activities are the best teaching tools. Thus, using some of the traditional Jewish activities in the celebration may be appropriate. But simply setting the appointed times aside each year to teach about them could suffice. Celebrating their Messianic implications seems an important element as well.

I believe that if churches were to begin to plan their church calendars around God's Appointed Times, they would find it extraordinarily energizing and exciting. God is the best artist at drawing a picture of Himself and His work to redeem mankind. Why not follow His program? As we will see in another chapter, the feasts are a prophetic timeline. It would result in a single church calendar, which would promote unity across all congregations and denominations.

Imagine the power of God that would be released if the entire

Body of Christ, worldwide, set the Day of Atonement aside each year to fast, pray, and gather together, repenting of individual, community, and national sin. I can think of at least one individual who can – that is why he is so intent on blinding believers to the value and meaning of God's Appointed Times to the Church.

Provoking the Jews to Jealousy

Moreover, bringing back our lost heritage in the feasts will have the added benefit of provoking the Jews to jealousy. This latter purpose is extremely important in the context of the One New Man. I've mentioned provoking the Jews to jealousy at least two times already. So a further explanation is in order because it is a key point for us to consider when discussing celebrating the feasts.

In the early part of his letter to the Romans, Paul states that the Gospel is to the Jew first and also to the Gentile. In Romans, chapters nine to eleven, the Apostle Paul extensively discusses the relationship between the salvation of the Jews and the Gentiles. There he lays out God's plan for making redemption available to all mankind, regardless of race or past spiritual heritage. But he emphasizes the original beneficiaries of the promise were the root-stock – the Jewish people.

It is here that the Lord speaks to us through Paul about the importance of provoking the Jewish people to "jealousy." Specifically, Romans 11:11-14 says:

> I say then, have they stumbled that they should fall [beyond redemption]? Certainly not! But through their fall, to **provoke them to jealousy**, salvation *has come* to the Gentiles. Now if their fall [means] riches for the world, and their failure riches for the Gentiles, how much more their fullness! For I speak to you Gentiles; inasmuch as I am an apostle to the

Gentiles, I magnify my ministry, if by any means I may **provoke to jealousy** *those who are* my flesh and save some of them. (KJV) (emphasis added).

Other translations use the phrase "to make Israel envious" (NIV) or "to make Israel jealous" (ESV). The point of these words is not the idea that we should try to annoy the Jewish people into recognizing their Messiah. Rather, the idea Paul is communicating is that we, as Gentiles, should not have an attitude of rejection and condescension towards the Jews, but rather, we should share the Gospel in such a way that they will desire to know the same kind of joy we have. We should carry out our worship and relate to them in such a manner that they will observe our walk, and worship of God, and be drawn to it.

Unfortunately, the opposite has been true in much of Church history. Rather than seeking to draw the Jewish people toward their Messiah, we have actually distanced ourselves from the Jewish roots of the faith and have rejected, and even persecuted, the Jewish people. This is the opposite of Paul's writings here and in other places in the New Testament.

In addition to Paul's written admonitions, Paul led by example. He repeatedly went first to the synagogue in any Gentile city to which he traveled to share the message of the Gospel.

The fact that the Church calendar and its main celebrations have been divorced from the Hebrew calendar and celebrations makes it all the more difficult to provoke Jews to jealousy. Our religion looks completely foreign to them. To most Jews, Gentile Christianity is completely unrecognizable to them as having ever been related to their religious belief system.

But imagine for a moment if Christians were celebrating the feasts in some manner and were conversant on their Messianic meaning and symbolism. What if Christians were aware of how

Jewish people celebrate the appointed times and what they believe the various elements mean? What if they could share the Gospel through their conversations with Jewish friends by being knowledgeable about the feasts?

The reality is that if you asked most Christians to share the Gospel through discussing the meaning of the feasts, they wouldn't even understand what you were proposing. They would struggle to relate in even a rudimentary way to Passover – the most obviously Messianic Appointed Time. However, if Christians were regularly celebrating the appointed times and receiving teaching on their Old Covenant purpose and their prophetic and New Covenant meaning in Messiah, consider what an amazing tool believers would carry for sharing the Gospel with Jewish people.

Additionally, as we Gentiles celebrate the feasts in the joy of the Holy Spirit, our participation in them – not out of dead legalism or because of tradition, but because of their meaning related to Jesus – will necessarily be attractive to Jewish people. It will, at the very least, raise a level of curiosity in them, because they have likely never seen Christians celebrating the feasts.

In fact, over the centuries, the Jews have generally only experienced persecution from Christians for their own celebration of God's Appointed Times. What a surprise it would be for them to see us celebrating with joy and inviting them to join us! This is another reason for Christians to celebrate the feasts. All the feasts are about relationship. Celebrating the feasts allows opportunity to invite Jewish people to our celebrations of them.

Indeed, over the past few years, I have led everything from a Shabbat dinner or Shabbat service to a full Passover Seder, and I have seen a number of Jewish people who have not yet accepted Jesus as Messiah attend these events. Most would never attend a church service. But they will attend a celebration of one of God's Appointed Times. More than occasionally, they have seemed in genuine disbelief that we are interested in the feasts, and even more surprised that we were welcoming them to participate with us.

Of course, celebrating the feasts requires us Gentiles to do a lot of learning and a lot of humbling ourselves so that we can show love in this way. We must be willing to surrender our way of doing things, so that, like Paul, we can "become all things to all men."

Christians have betrayed Jewish people so many times in the past that Jewish people struggle with a high level of collective distrust of Christians. Only genuine love without an agenda will break through this barrier. Jesus invites people to believe in Him as Messiah. He doesn't condemn, guilt, or manipulate. Even today, most Jewish people associate Jesus with persecution because their ancestors were threatened with the penalty of death if they did not confess Jesus as Messiah.

Many Jewish people realize that modern-day Christians (particularly evangelicals) are more friendly to them than most other religions, but the generational memory of persecution and betrayal at the hands of Christians as recently as a few decades ago is never far from their minds. It is only by His Spirit, guiding believers to do this Divine work of restoration, that the One New Man will be realized.

21

They're All About Worship

At their core, the feasts are all about worshiping the Creator God and His son Jesus. Jesus must be the center of all worship or it will quickly become legalistic, lifeless, burdensome, and even enslaving.

As we noted in the last chapter, we often seek a list of rules to follow in leu of genuine relationship with Jesus. Rules allow us to rely on our own righteousness. But walking with the Lord in relationship demands we be vulnerable to the Lord and willing to obey His voice – which is always challenging to our fleshly desires and ways.

Because the feasts are appointments with the Lord, they are times to draw close to Him. He doesn't want them to be about the rules and regulations. He is our Father. As a good Father, He wants time with us. He made us to worship and bring glory to Him. But He also made us to walk and fellowship with Him. Our lives are most full of joy and peace when we are doing both.

One reason many Christians are closed to considering celebrating the Feasts of the Lord is that they wrongly believe that celebrating the feasts logically leads to a requirement that we live according to all the ceremonial laws of the Old Covenant. And they will quickly argue something like "we are not under the law but under grace." They fear coming "under law" and being bound by traditions which burden people and actually have the opposite effect from what God intended.

The teachers of the law in Jesus' day had perverted the Shabbat in this way. They had made God's people enslaved to rules and regulations about Shabbat which actually blocked, rather than facilitated, the personal relationship with God that Shabbat was created to encourage. The religious leaders had imposed rules that actually prevented Jesus from healing on the Sabbath. This illustrates the damaging effects of focusing on behaviors instead of beliefs and attitudes of the heart.

I recall one Messianic group I was familiar with moving toward more and more legalistic behaviors and attitudes about matters that the Bible clearly teaches are matters of conscience. Soon they were denying that Jesus is God.

During a meeting with this group, while I was raising various Scriptures that unequivocally prove that Jesus claimed to be, and was in fact, God, my wife suddenly interrupted the debate and asked one very simple question: "So you don't talk or pray to Jesus?" One man instantly answered with an air of indignation: "We only pray to God!" My wife responded with a genuine sadness that I believe was coming from the Lord's heart: "That makes me sad," she said. "I don't know what I would do if I couldn't talk to Jesus." The room suddenly fell silent.

That's a profound truth. Jesus is the intercessor between God and man. It is through His work on the Cross that we are able to have any relationship with the Father. Legalism dispenses with our need for Jesus and makes our righteousness sufficient to reconcile us to God – or so we believe. But it is only through the Spirit of Jesus that we can know and understand God's will and properly interpret His written Word.

In the same way, Jesus taught that Shabbat was all about Him. He demonstrated that Shabbat was made for man and not man for Shabbat. In Matthew 12:1-4 and 23:4, Jesus rebuked this religious and legalistic spirit that missed the whole point of Shabbat. "Take my yoke upon you," Jesus said, "for my yoke is easy and my burden is light."

Jesus is Lord of the Sabbath and Jesus was all about compassion, love, gentleness, kindness, humility, and putting others before Himself. This is a good rule of thumb when celebrating the feasts or engaging in any kind of worship to the Lord. Is the worship enslaving or freeing? Is it heavy and burdensome or refreshing and light?

This is not to dismiss the need for discipline in our spiritual walk. The Lord says many times in the Scriptures not to forget His commands. Jesus urged the disciples (and by extension us) to watch and pray so that we do not fall into temptation. God told us to set His laws and teachings before our eyes and to walk in the ways of righteousness.

But His laws are sweet. They are refreshing. They are rewarding – if they are practiced and followed as an expression of worship to who Jesus is and not an effort to buy His approval or be more righteous than the next guy.

The laws and guidelines God has given man emanate from His character and nature. We are created in His image, so we have an innate need to live according to God's moral laws in order to be at peace. God gave us the guidelines of the law because He was the Devine Designer of the human being. We are a reflection of who He is, and He therefore knew we needed to follow these guidelines to be at peace. So God's laws are good for us to keep, but they cannot make us righteous. They cannot create a relationship with God.

In the same way, the feasts of the Lord are good for us to celebrate in some fashion. They are times on God's calendar when He wants to have an appointment with us. But we do not have to approach God in the same way as the Israelites did before Jesus came. They could only have relationship if proper sacrifices and protocols were exactly performed and followed.

Because we have Jesus, we don't have to worry about the letter of those laws. The blood of Jesus and His death on the cross made a way for us to have fellowship with Him. Now we can worship Him with clean hearts and not have to perform rituals in order to approach Him in worship.

So this is really what any observance of the feasts should be about. The Lord wants us to engage in them with a heart of worship for who He is, what He has done, what He is doing, and what He will do in the future.

The Unifying Nature of Worship

When people worship Jesus together, I have seen many walls come down. Provided that the participants are not legalistically critiquing the style of worship and/or legalistically restricting freedom and variety in the approaches and styles of worship, worship draws people together.

Music is one type of worship that universally connects people. It is a powerful unifier for both good and evil. In fact, many of the arts can bring joy and unity to people from vastly divergent cultural and racial backgrounds.

The feasts are expressions of worship to the Lord and, as such, they can serve to unify people from vastly diverse backgrounds. This is particularly true if freedom in how the feasts are observed is permitted. This raises an important truth about the feasts that is unavoidable as we see more and more Jewish people recognize and begin to worship Jesus as their Messiah.

How Shall They be One?

The feasts were given to the Jews as a lasting memorial throughout their generations forever. The Scripture is clear about this, for example it says regarding Passover:

> And this day shall be unto you for a memorial; and ye shall keep it a feast to the LORD throughout your generations; ye shall keep it a feast by an ordinance forever. (KJV) (Exodus 12:14)[37]

If the feasts are only for the Jews or Messianic Jewish believers and not for Gentile believers, but the Jews are charged with celebrating them "forever," how will Gentile and Jewish believers ever become one as Jesus prayed in John 17? If the Jews that come to faith in Jesus continue to engage in the feasts and we Gentile believers tenaciously refuse to engage in the feasts because they seem foreign or they are not our Christian traditions, how can we ever become one with our Jewish brothers and sisters that have come to faith in Jesus?

This is another key reason that Gentile believers should embrace celebrating the feasts. Scripture makes clear that the Jews must engage with the feasts if they are to fulfill God's directives. Even if we reject that they are part of a Christians' inheritance, unity between Messianic Jews and Christian Gentiles of the kind prayed for by Jesus will be impossible if we refuse to join them.

22

The Feasts as a Prophetic Timeline

The feasts are a prophetic timeline. This may be one of the most significant reasons God is reintroducing the Church to His Appointed Times in this particular season. We've seen that each feast represents one significant part of Jesus' plan for redemption of mankind, but the fall feasts have not been prophetically fulfilled and won't be until the End Times.

In the spring feasts we see that Jesus died on Passover, raised on Firstfruits, and gave His Holy Spirit on Shavuot. He fulfilled the relevant feasts consecutively and to the day. If He fulfilled the spring feasts in this manner, why wouldn't He do the same in fulfilling the fall feasts?

I have always found eschatology to be confusing and seemingly contradictory. Having grown up being taught Dispensationalism, which included pre-Millennialism and a pre-Tribulation Rapture, I found scholarly efforts to harmonize the New Testament and Old Testament prophecies wanting. I later heard and read Postmillennial and Amillennial views of End Time prophecy and they left me similarly baffled.

Despite sitting under very intelligent and well-studied professors in Bible college and seminary and reading numerous books and hearing countless sermons, none of the teaching I heard on this subject served to harmonize the chronology of the Time of Jacob's Trouble, the Jewish return to the land of Israel, The Great Tribulation, the Rapture, Jesus' return, the binding of satan, the Millennial Kingdom, the release of satan, the Great White Throne Judgment, the second death, the establishment of the New Heavens and the New Earth, etc. It seemed to me that the Church had created different theologies of the end times into which they struggled mightily to fit prophecy.

When it dawned on me that Jesus had fulfilled the spring feasts on the daily calendar in rapid succession on the day of the appointed times representing His first advent, it suddenly made perfect sense that He would fulfill the fall feasts in the same manner.

The fall feasts create a framework for our prophetic puzzle. If we understand the prophetic meaning of each feast, and that those events are fulfilled within 15 days of one another, we can harmonize them with the prophecies of the Old and New Testaments. We can then build a more meaningful and clear picture of the prophetic implications of the individual fall feasts, while at the same time clarifying the timeline of End Time events recorded in the Old and New Testaments.

Just as individual jigsaw puzzle pieces don't make sense apart from their surrounding pieces, and building the frame of the puzzle is a good strategy to "solving" the puzzle, so using the feasts as a prophetic puzzle framework for the End Times helps us fit the other pieces into a cogent and recognizable whole.

This doesn't solve all our challenges with understanding prophecy that has yet to be fulfilled. Some confusion regarding the prophetic timeline of the End Times necessarily comes from the reality that the full meaning of prophecy is never clear until the prophesied events occur. Only then can we look back at the prophecy and see that it was fulfilled and how the original language of the prophecy specifically related to the ultimate fulfillment. Hindsight in interpreting prophecy is, as in other things, 20/20.

For example, when Jesus came the first time, many were confused because they didn't understand or ignored the Messianic prophecies that presented Jesus as a suffering servant. They'd focused on the happier thought of the Messiah coming as the conquering King. I've heard many Christian sermons seemingly belittle the Jews for missing this, but I wonder if we Christians are doing any better with the End Times prophecies about Jesus' return.

Another confusion among people who were genuinely looking for the first advent of Messiah was over where Messiah would come from. Because He grew up in Nazareth, many "prophecy scholars" of Jesus day dismissed Him as the Messiah. Who could have predicted that Jesus would be born in Bethlehem, move to Egypt, and grow up in Nazareth, fulfilling several seemingly contradictory prophecies that wouldn't be discerned fully until He fulfilled them?

So I don't believe that anyone will figure out all the End Times prophecies before Jesus actually fulfills them. All believers "look through a darkened glass," as Paul describes it, regarding issues in the future.

Nevertheless, prophecy is fairly useless if it leaves us with such potentially divergent possible scenarios that it's impossible to look to the prophecy for any guidance regarding what is to come. The New Testament makes it clear that the wise men from the east knew that the birth of a king was coming, and they knew where and approximately when it was going to happen. They understood the signs in the heavens and had read prophetic writings.

I also believe that the Lord will raise up modern-day prophets in the End Times who will receive greater and greater clarity on the meaning of the prophecies and may even receive revelation from angels and the Holy Spirit that, when tested against the written Word of God, provided we know and understand it fully, will confirm the truth of what they believe they have received from the Lord.

It also seems likely that if we don't have a greater understanding of the End Times prophecies by the time they are upon us, there will be many deceptions released. In fact, the more divorced believers are from their Old Covenant roots, the more likely they will be to be led away into error and deception by demonic forces assigned to that task. By contrast, those that have embraced the Old Covenant and the role the Jewish people hold in God's End Time's prophecy will see clearly into these deceptions and distortions.

In any event, we should be able to read the Old Testament prophecies and have them inform and direct our understanding of Jesus' Second Coming. Add to that picture the things Jesus taught about His return and what was written by Paul, Peter, and John in the New Testament, and we should have at least as clear a picture of how things will progress just before and when Jesus returns as faithful people, like Simeon and Anna, had at time of His first appearance.

Part of the challenge to the Church's interpretation of prophecy comes from Christians' ignorance of the Old Testament in its Jewish context. That is a consequence of the Church fathers cutting the Church off from its Jewish identity as we have seen in earlier chapters. In doing so, they were forced to spiritualize many Old Testament prophecies to support their replacement theology. This in turn convoluted the prophecies as they related to the Second Coming and the End Times.

But applying the principle that the events pictured in the fall feasts will happen in rapid succession and within 15 days of each other, we have a much more solid framework within which to piece together the various bits of the End Times prophetic puzzle. If we are using this framework to build our prophetic picture, we have a better chance of interpreting prophetic events effectively.

The Rapture will happen, but the time that will elapse between the Rapture and Jesus' touchdown on the Mount of Olives will be a matter of days and not years. During that time the nations and Israel will "look on Him whom [we] pierced" and mourn for Him. (Zech. 12:10; Rev. 1:7)

Using the fall feasts as a guide, it makes sense that the dead and the living believers will be caught up to meet Jesus in the heavens at the final trump but will, within 10 days, return to the earth with Jesus to judge the nations for their treatment of Israel. Five days after that, the inauguration of Jesus as King of the whole earth will occur during the great celebration of Sukkot. The cry of "Lord Save Us!" at Sukkot celebrations over thousands of years will be a reality! I believe this will be the Marriage Supper of the Lamb when the Body of redeemed believers in Jesus will be married to Jesus as His bride. We will become one with Him in a spiritual sense in the same way that Adam was in relationship with the Lord.

Believers who were raptured or raised from the dead will have glorified bodies in which they will rule and reign with Jesus. They will serve as His emissaries and will help Him set up the Millennial Kingdom on earth. They will be able to translate from place to place (like Jesus did in His glorified body), walk through walls and perform all manner of miraculous works that currently would seem impossible but will be commonplace in the Millennial Kingdom. Satan and his demons will be bound during this time, so temptation to sin, theoretically, won't exist.

Once the Millennium comes to an end, the devil and his minions will be released once again to tempt people who have been born during the Millennium. Some will stay faithful to God and others will rebel just as Adam did. The final judgment will take place where all people, living and dead, will be examined in light of the Lamb's Book of Life. The Millennium will end with the destruction of satan and all humanity who have rebelled against God, and the Lord will establish the New Heavens and the New Earth, with the New Jerusalem.

Even in the feast of Passover, we can see a reflection of the plagues that will be brought upon the earth during the time of Revelation. I believe we can expect that believers who are living at the time of the Great Tribulation will enjoy protection in places the Lord is preparing that only believers will be able to locate or access. Just as the Lord covered the Israelites in Goshen, so He will cover the believers in these places of refuge. Just as God covered Noah in an ark, the Lord will provide arks of safety from the outpouring of His judgment on the earth.

Paul says in I Corinthians 15 that we will be caught up to be with the Lord "at the last trump". Could that hearken to the seventh trumpet of judgement in Revelation? Perhaps the rapture of the believers happens after the seventh trumpet but before the bowl judgments which theoretically would occur during the ten days between Trumpets and Day of Atonement?

On the Day of Atonement, the people remaining on the earth repent and the Lord relents. Satan is bound and cast into the lake of fire and the Lord touches down on the Mount of Olives and begins His Millennial reign as described above.

Thus, we see that the feasts at least give us a solid framework of time to use in interpreting the prophetic timeline for the cataclysmic events which will happen around the Lord's Second Coming.

Although more thought and consideration needs to be given to exactly how the fall feasts will be fulfilled at Jesus' Second Coming,

I believe a strong argument can be made that they will be fulfilled within the literal 22-day calendar period just as the spring feasts were fulfilled in the literal 53-day period during Jesus' first advent.

23

Put Yourself in the Sheet

When the Lord first revealed to me the importance of Israel to the Church and His related End Times purposes at the conference in Blackpool, England, in 2009, the Lord directed me to kneel in the sheet that they had laid out at the conference to collect an offering for Israel. I believe this is symbolic of the call the Lord is giving to the broader Church at this time. He's asking us if we are willing to leave our comfort zone, step outside of our respective boxes, and make the sacrifices necessary to facilitate the realization of the One New Man.

Christians often resist the message about the feasts for one or more of the following reasons: 1) they simply don't know about them or understand that they are relevant to Christians; 2) they see them as "laws" or "burdens" and dismiss engagement with them as "coming under the law;" or 3) they believe if they participate in or engage with them that they are "becoming Jewish."

As we have seen, none of these "spiritual scarecrows" that the enemy has erected are genuine issues. The feasts are relevant to Christians, they are a blessing and not a burden, and engaging with them does not make a Gentile believer Jewish. Since they're Jesus' Appointed Times, the feasts simply identify them as followers of Jesus.

Familiarity with, and participation in, the Feasts of the Lord, is part of God's divine plan to bring the Jewish people to the recognition of Jesus as Messiah and to reconnect the Gentile Church to its identity in the Old Covenant and her Jewish heritage. The Lord emphasized this to me very clearly through two instances that happened during a visit to Israel in 2017. I will start with the second event first.

In 2017, the Lord very clearly told me to travel to Israel during the Feast of Tabernacles. He told me I must arrive before the seventh day of Sukkot, known as Hoshana Rabah – the day religious Jews go to their synagogue, or, in the case of religious Jews in Jerusalem, to the Western Wall. During this gathering, religious Jews waive the Lulav and shout "Hoshana, Hoshana." He instructed me to go to the Western Wall and participate in this ceremony which occurs at sunrise on the seventh day of Sukkot.

I will tell you more about that day when I share the second encounter. But I will first share what happened on the Eighth day of Sukkot. The Eighth day is called Simchat Torah, and the Jewish people celebrate the blessing of the Torah (even though they recognize that it was actually given on Shavuot). On this day of Sukkot, which is always a Shabbat as commanded in Leviticus 23, various groups of religious Jews go to the Western Wall and do various ceremonies, readings, and prayers dictated by which rabbi they follow. But one nearly universal activity on Simchat Torah, engaged in by adherents to all "stripes" of Judaism, is dancing with the Torah.

At the Western Wall, on Simchat Torah, you will see many groups of Jewish men carrying the Torah and dancing in circles while singing and rejoicing. The morning of the eighth day, the Lord told me to go back to the Western Wall where I had been the day before. He told me to sit and read the Bible and pray.

When I opened my Bible, it fell open to Nehemiah 8. I began to read, and this is what it said:

> On the second day of the month, the heads of all the families, along with the priests and the Levites, gathered around Ezra the teacher to give attention to the words of the Law. They found written in the Law, which the Lord had commanded through Moses, that the Israelites were to live in temporary shelters during the festival of the seventh month and that they should proclaim this word and spread it throughout their towns and in Jerusalem: "Go out into the hill country and bring back branches from olive and wild olive trees, and from myrtles, palms and shade trees, to make temporary shelters"—as it is written. So the people went out and brought back branches and built themselves temporary shelters on their own roofs, in their courtyards, in the courts of the house of God and in the square by the Water Gate and the one by the Gate of Ephraim. The whole company that had returned from exile built temporary shelters and lived in them. From the days of Joshua son of Nun until that day, the Israelites had not celebrated it like this. And their joy was very great. Day after day, from the first day to the last, Ezra read from the Book of the Law of God. They celebrated the festival for seven days, and on the eighth day, in accordance with the regulation, there was an assembly. (Neh. 8:13-18) (NIV)

Amazingly, I was reading about Sukkot and the eighth day of Sukkot while I was in Israel at the place of the ancient Temple where Nehemiah and the people were celebrating the same festival. I was now witnessing it being celebrated in the same place by the Jewish people in 2017, thousands of years after the people of Nehemiah's time. The text makes it clear that the people of Israel had stopped celebrating the Feast of Tabernacles like this, and they were rediscovering it. This rediscovery brough great joy and celebration.

As I looked to my left, a group of Jewish men were becoming extra joyful in the dance with the Torah. The Lord said very clearly: "I want Christians and Jews to trade dance partners. I want Gentile believers to 'dance' with the Torah. I want the Jewish people to 'dance' with Me."

His meaning was clear to me. What I understood Him to be saying was, "I want you Gentile believers to get to know and understand Me as the God of the Old Covenant (Torah). I want the Jews to know Me as the God of the New Covenant (Jesus and My Holy Spirit)." Wow! What an amazing revelation. The feasts would serve as a means to reconnect each of us to the root identity of who God is in all three Persons of the Trinity and as revealed in the Torah.

The second story I will share from that trip to Israel in 2017 actually happened first, chronologically. The morning after I arrived in Israel, was Hoshana Rabah. After I spent about three hours early on Hoshana Rabbah waving the Lulav and praying at the Western Wall, I returned to my guest house to take a nap. When I awoke, I asked the Lord what He wanted me to do next. He instructed me to return to the Western Wall.

As I walked through the parking lot on my way to enter the Zion Gate of the Old City of Jerusalem, heading toward the Western Wall, a lady shouted in my direction, in Hebrew. I looked at her and it was obvious she was talking to me. I responded that I didn't speak Hebrew. She immediately began to speak English. She asked me the way to the "Kotel," which is the Israeli or Jewish name for the Western Wall. I immediately thought how ironic it was that a Jewish Israeli woman was asking a Christian foreigner the way to the holiest Jewish site in Israel.

Nevertheless, I told her I was on my way to the Western Wall and invited her to simply follow me, I would take her there. She thanked me but declined to accept, saying something about being an old woman and having to walk slowly. She didn't want to slow me down. She also had a young boy with her, who I later came to understand was her grandson of about 12 years old.

As I turned to continue on my way to the Western Wall, immediately, the Lord said, "Do not leave her." I turned back toward the parking lot. I was now on the steps leading up to the Zion gate. I began to address the lady again and engage her in conversation. She was now climbing the steps below me.

Anyone who has been in Jerusalem knows how the lime-stone used on the steps and streets of the Old City and other areas in Jerusalem is often worn down and can become very slick when wet. It had just lightly rained. When this elderly Jewish lady took her next step, she suddenly slipped and fell hard on the limestone stairs. Her cane clattered to the ground and her body made a sickening thud as she struck the unforgiving rocks.

Another man in the parking lot ran to help me lift her up to her feet. She muttered something about probably not being able to go to the Kotel after all. When she had regained her composure, she indicated that she would continue to the Kotel. Over her objections, I insisted that I walk with her. Still objecting that she would hold me up too much on my journey, we began to walk together through the Zion gate and made our way down toward the Western Wall.

As we walked, she told me about her family. She shared that the grandson who was with her was going to have his bar mitzvah at the Western Wall. This was the reason they had driven from Tel

Aviv to Jerusalem that day. As we walked and talked together, the Holy Spirit began to speak to me. He reminded me of Paul's words in Romans 11: "Have they [the Jews] fallen so that they cannot get up?" Paul's answer: "Absolutely not!" In fact, Paul said the Jewish people will return to the Lord and recognize Jesus as the Messiah. The Lord's point to me was clear.

Just as I had helped this Jewish lady stand back up and in the same manner that I was walking her very slowly back to the ancient place of worship where the Temple once stood, so were Christians to be helping the Jewish people stand to their spiritual feet and return to the place of worshiping the true and living God as manifested in Messiah Jesus. He made clear to me that day that we cannot rush the Jewish people back to this place of worship. We must walk with them slowly. We must get to know them and understand them and their family histories and the struggles they have endured. This cannot be a religious effort or an attempt to make "spiritual points." It has to be motivated by and done in genuine, Spirit-filled, love.

Surprisingly, when we arrived at the Western Wall, the family invited me to join them in the celebration of the grandson's bar mitzvah. At one point, I was helping the boy's father put the tallit on the grandson according to the traditional way of folding and wearing it. Again, I found it ironic that I would be helping a Jewish person put on their garments of worship.

Afterward, they invited me to join them for dinner. We found a place to eat near the Jaffa gate but were quickly driven out by the Arab proprietor because they were Jewish. Because it was already late afternoon on the seventh day of Sukkot, the following day, the eighth day, was a Shabbat and all restaurants managed by Jews were beginning to close. I noticed the coffee shop at Christ Church – the oldest Protestant church building in the Middle East – was open. I suggested we go there. As I sat and talked with the family, the kids ran into the courtyard area of the church complex. They soon returned and said to their parents excitedly in Hebrew: "The court-yard is like heaven; it is beautiful and peaceful."

I had been in that courtyard many times. Although it was nice, I wouldn't describe it as heaven. I suddenly realized that these Jewish children were experiencing the presence and peace of the Holy Spirit.

In that encounter, the Lord had demonstrated to me His heart in this whole matter of the One New Man. The Lord wants us to receive something of a deposit of His heart for the Jewish people and be willing to do whatever it takes to help them return to the place of worship of the one true and living God by recognizing Jesus as their Messiah.

Restoring the One New Man

The crux of the entire matter of bringing the One New Man to healing and health as a unified body lies with the Church being willing to go to the place where brokenness happened and deal with it through repentance and reconciliation. The One New Man cannot function in wholeness and health as long as unresolved brokenness remains in it – even if that breaking happened centuries and even Millennia in the past.

The Church's rejection of our identity with Israel, the Jewish people, and the Old Covenant has precipitated disunity within the Church, that has only grown over the centuries. We cannot be fully blessed in unity among ourselves as Gentile believers, let alone with our Jewish believing brothers and sisters, until we have addressed the brokenness inflicted when the Church rejected its Jewish and Old Covenant identity.

Repentance and asking forgiveness of God and the Jewish people for our rejection of them is very important in the process of healing our relationship with the Jewish people and restoring a broken part of our relationship with God. And I applaud those that are taking the lead to encourage the Church to do this. This was and is important and necessary for healing.

But more important than even the activity of repenting and asking forgiveness for antisemitism is restoring the worship practices that, although God-ordained, were rejected and abandoned simply because they were associated with the Jewish people.

As we begin to align ourselves again with the Old Covenant and the Jewish people, I believe our obedience will release His Spirit of conviction on those who have yet to believe in Yeshua as Messiah. In the last decade, we have seen an unprecedented movement of Jewish people coming to know their Messiah. Most attest to supernatural events like dreams and visions drawing them to seek out the truth about Jesus. It has always been God's plan that the Jews would bring the message of salvation to the Gentiles and the Gentiles would bring that message back to the Jews when the time of the Gentiles reached its fullness.

I have often thought of the great struggles and hardships Paul suffered in order to bring the Gospel to the Gentiles. He was misunderstood and rejected by not only those Jews who had rejected Jesus as Messiah, but also by those Jews who had accepted Him. More than once he had to defend his actions in taking the Gospel to the Gentiles, and against allegations that he was perverting God's Word or teaching some new heretical doctrine.

The question the Lord is posing to us Gentile believers in this generation is, "Are you willing to suffer even as Paul did to take the Gospel full circle back to the Jewish people? Are you prepared to deal with the opposition and misunderstanding of not only the Jewish people you are trying to love, but also those among your own ranks as Gentile believers who do not understand why you are doing what you are doing? Are you willing to be considered weird or out of the mainstream to accomplish God's most important Kingdom purposes in your generation? Are you willing to be the living sacrifices Paul exhorts believers to be in Romans 12:1 so that the Lord will be glorified by the return of His chosen people to true faith in Him and His Messiah, Jesus?"

I believe we have entered that season when the fullness of the Gentiles has come and the veil is falling from the Jewish people's eyes. God is now challenging us to look beyond our selfish ways and see His important Kingdom purposes in restoring the feasts to the Church and, through that, drawing the Jewish people to their Messiah. The question is: Are we willing to sacrifice our comfort to step out into God's Kingdom plans? Are we willing to put ourselves in the offering sheet?

Appendix 1

Prayers Regarding Antisemitism

Lord Jesus, I confess that You are both my Savior and the Lord of my life. I invite You now to bring to my mind any occasion when I have strayed from Your truth, consciously or unconsciously, as the result of my upbringing: in my family, in my church or from anyone who has deceived me.

Confession of Personal Antisemitism

I acknowledge Your covenant with Abraham, Isaac, and Jacob, to whom You promised descendants, a chosen nation to be a light to the nations, a people You call the *"apple of Your eye."* I also acknowledge the work of satan to destroy Your chosen nation.

I ask You to forgive me for any words or deeds that I have said or committed against Your people, the Jews...................... (pause: confess to the Lord any particular instance you can recall).

Confession of Family Antisemitism

Lord Jesus, if there is any antisemitism that has passed down the generations of my family, I ask You to forgive our family iniquity and I forgive my ancestors for any curse and damage it has brought in the generational line and in my life. Specifically, I forgive

.... (pause: quietly speak out the name and forgiveness of any specific family member to which it applies)

Please break any ungodly tie from this between me and any of my family line.

Confession of Antisemitism in Spiritual Family Line

Lord Jesus, if there is any wrong teaching I have received regarding Your people Israel: that the church now replaces Israel in Your purposes; that You have cursed every generation of the Jews for killing Jesus; that the Jews are an example of people who will never be saved; that all Your blessings and promises are now exclusively for the Church; that the Old Testament is inferior to the New Testament,

I forgive my pastors/ministers/teachers for their misguided teaching and its consequences in my life. Specifically, I forgive .... (pause: name any specific occasions and persons you can recall).

Please break every ungodly tie between me and them.

Please set me free from these deceptions that I may fully receive the truth of Your Word.

In Jesus' Name, I break all curses of antisemitism over my life that have come from my own antisemitism, my ancestors' antisemitism, or my agreement and connection to antisemitic spiritual leaders or teachings.

In Jesus' Name I command all spirits of antisemitism to leave me now. (pause in silence – is the Lord speaking to you?)

Thank You that I am washed clean in Your blood, Lord Jesus. Thank You that You have won the victory over death and hell, and in You I have life in all its fullness.

Prayers Regarding Rejecting Identity in Israel

I forgive every person or group of people that tortured, abused, murdered, stole, rejected or otherwise sinned against me or my ancestors because of our identity in Israel or for being Jewish. I release and forgive each and every one of those who have hurt me directly or through my ancestors. Specifically, I forgive ______.

I forgive those who have offended me because of their behavior, beliefs or culture as a Jewish person, including my own Jewish family or ancestors.

I forgive all these people for any way they caused me to reject my identity as a descendant of Israel or my inheritance in both the land of Israel and the people of Israel. I specifically forgive __________ (name any person or people group you know or suspect negatively affected your decision to identify as a descendant of Israel or as Jewish).

I ask You to forgive me for rejecting my own identity in Israel and any way I agreed with the enemy about this and for taking on any false identity that rejected my true calling and purpose.

I ask now that You would break and sever every ungodly soul tie between me and any of those who caused me to reject my identity in Israel.

In Yeshua's name, I command anything of satan that has held me in bondage, preventing me from coming into the fullness of my identity, to leave me now, never to return.

Father God, I now choose to accept what You say is my identity, and all that means for me and my family in Your Kingdom. Please show me how to walk in who You say I am so that I bring the unity among Your children that You seek.

Thank You that as a Gentile or Jew I too am chosen as You have said, Lord Jesus, *"You did not choose me, but I chose you and appointed you to go and bear fruit – fruit that will last."* (John 15:16). Thank You for the privilege and responsibility of being chosen.

In Jesus' name I pray. Amen!

Appendix 2

Ways Christians May Wish to Celebrate God's Appointed Times

Passover – Attend a Messianic Jewish Passover Seder with a Messianic synagogue or ministry. If you can't locate one near you, hold a Passover Seder in your home for your family and friends. Obtain a Messianic Jewish Haggadah and use it to walk through the Passover elements and the telling of the Exodus. Incorporate any elements that recognize Jesus as the Lamb of God and connect the celebration you are holding to the first Passover during Israel's Exodus from Egypt. Following are some links to Messianic Haggadahs (order for the prayers and activities of Passover, that include prayers and teaching):

- https://www.olivetreemessianic.org/uploads/1/6/7/5/16753254/weebly_copy_of_the_passover_haggadah_04-08-17.pdf
- http://streamsinthenegev.com/wp-content/uploads/2011/02/sedereng.pdf
- https://www.chosenpeople.com/wp-content/uploads/2021/03/Messianic-Passover-Haggadah.pdf

Firstfruits – Celebrate Firstfruits during your Passover Seder on the eve of Passover or hold a prayer meeting to remember Jesus' resurrection the day after Passover. You could celebrate Passover on Firstfruits and combine them as a single event. The key is to recognize that the barley being lifted up represented Jesus' resurrection as the Firstfruits of many to be raised from the dead.

Feast of Unleavened bread – You might choose to remove all leaven form your home and abstain from eating it for the week of this feast. Our family typically does not abstain from eating things containing yeast or limit ourselves to matzah in lieu of bread. But we have fasted something else during that week. We've also prayed through our home and asked the Lord to reveal any "spiritual leaven" in the home and have prayed over and disposed of anything He's shown us that we shouldn't have.

Shavuot – Hold a special evening worship service and celebrate the Word and the Holy Spirit. We've done a variety of different things to celebrate Shavuot. We have had all night prayer meetings or a 24-hour prayer watch during Shavuot. We always have worship and praise and typically Messianic style dancing at the services we hold. We've held special teaching weekends on or near Shavuot about the Ministry of the Holy Spirit. Anything that recognizes and connects to the giving of the Holy Spirit and the preciousness of the Word of God could be included in your celebration of Shavuot. We've read through the book of Ruth, which is a tradition in Jewish Synagogues, on Shavuot.

Trumpets – We hold an evening service and blow shofars and talk about the Second Coming of Jesus. It can be a celebratory time. But it can also be a more solemn time, because you are entering into the Days of Awe just before the Day of Atonement. We often teach about the feasts on the feast days because that is part of God's personal call for us. Jewish people celebrate Trumpets with apples and honey to signify a sweet new year, because they are celebrating the Jewish civil new year on the Feast of Trumpets.

Day of Atonement – When our children were still living with us, we kept them home from school and we fasted from sundown the evening before the Day of Atonement until sundown on the Day of Atonement. We spent time reading the Word and spending time as a family at home. We often napped in the afternoon because, when fasting, sleep in the afternoon of the first day of a fasting is necessary. We broke the fast together, as a family, as the sun set on the Day of Atonement. In recent years, as more people are recognizing and participating in the feasts, we have held services on the eve of the Day of Atonement and at sunset on the Day of Atonement. Those who attend the second service either break the fast together, wherever we are meeting, or we break the fast at a local restaurant. I use a liturgy composed of prayers, Scripture readings, and confessions drawn from Messianic Jewish liturgies. These are responsive readings between the leader and congregation.

Sukkot – While our children were young, we built a personal sukkah in our back yard for many years. Now we build a sukkah at our ministry each year. We invite friends and family to come and fellowship with us in the Sukkah throughout the week. We often hold teaching events about Sukkot and include a workshop that has the participants build and decorate their own Sukkah and visit each other's Sukkahs. We dance and celebrate with music and palm fronds.

Appendix 3

Additional Reading

Brown, Michael. *Our Hands are Stained with Blood.* Shippensburg, PA: Destiny Image Publishers, Inc., 2019.

Crombie, Kevin. *For the Love of Zion.* Bristol, UK: Terra Nova Publications International, 2008.

Finto, Don 2001. *Your People Shall Be My People.* Bloomington, MN: Chosen Books, 2001.

Francis, William. *Celebrate the Feasts of the Lord.* Alexandria, VA: Crest Books, 2012

Howard, Kevin and Marvin Rosenthal. *The Feasts of the Lord.* Nashville, TN: Thomas Nelson, 1997.

Intrater, Keith and Dan Juster. *Israel the Church and the Last Days.* Shippensburg, PA: Destiny Image Publishers, Inc., 2003.

Prince, Derek. *The Destiny of Israel and the Church.* Charlotte, NC: Derek Prince Ministries-International, 2007.

Scott, Bruce. *The Feasts of Israel.* Bellmawr, NJ: The Friends of Israel Gospel Ministry, Inc., 1993.

Teplinsky, Sandra. *Why Care about Israel?* Ada, MI: Chosen Books, 2004.

Zimmerman, Martha. *Celebrating Biblical Feast In Your Home or Church.* Bloomington, MN: Bethany House Publishers, 2004.

End Notes

1. Accepting our family history and inheritance does not mean we must dress like our ancestors and behave in every way as they did. Do we need to identify with our ancestors by wearing their style of clothing and celebrating all our holidays exactly the way they did? Of course not! This is why the Apostle Paul talks about a circumcision of the heart and not the imposition of the identity by outward physical appearance.

2. Throughout this book I will use the term Messiah, Jesus, and Yeshua interchangeably. All mean the same person – Jesus of Nazareth who came in the flesh and died as an atoning sacrifice for our sins.

3. A Seder is a special meal, often on the Eve of Passover, that celebrates the children of Israel coming out of Egypt. For believers in Jesus, it also relates to Jesus' death, burial, and resurrection. This meal is something like the meal the Lord held with the disciples before his crucifixion – what Christians commonly call "the Last Supper." Seder simply means "order" or "procedure" referring to the order of the meal with its symbolic elements and related prayers and worship.

4. *Status of Global Mission, 2014, in the Context of AD 1800–2025*. Retrieved September 13, 2015 from http://www.gordonconwell.edu/resources/documents/StatusOfGlobalMission.pdf

5. *Id.*

6. Hay, Malcom (1984). *The Roots of Christian Anti-Semitism.* (Emphasis added.)

7. *Id.* (Emphasis added).

8. *Id. See also,* Brown, Michael L. (1990), *Our Hands are Stained with Blood,* p. 10. Destiny Image Publishers. Shippensburg, PA. (Emphasis added.)

9. *The Letter of the Synod in Nicea to the Egyptians.* Retrieved on September 13, 2015, from http://www.papalencyclicals.net/Councils/ecum01.htm

10.   *Early Church History*, CH101, Retrieved July 18, 2019 from www.church-history101.com/century4-p7.php (emphasis added).

11.   Maseko, A. N. (2008). *Church Schisms and Corruption*, p.47. Retrieved from https://books.google.com.

12.   *Eusebius Pamphilius: Church History, Life of Constantine, Oration in Praise of Constantine* Retrieved from www.ccel.org/ccel/schaff/ npnf201.iv.vi.iii.xviii.html

13.   Maseko at 47 (citing Jackson, Blomfield. *The Ecclesiastical History, Dialogues, and Letters of Theodoret*. Retrieved on 2006-05-08)

14.   Lazare, Bernard (1894). *Anti-Semitism Its History and Causes*, p. 30. Retrieved July 18, 2019 from http://www.jrbooksonline.com/ PDF_Books_added2009-4/antisemitismcauses.pdf.

15.   Appointed Times of God – Divine Seasons [Power Point Slides], slide 43. Retrieved from http://www.slideshare.net/acyulo/gods-appointed-time-part-2. *See also*, Cohn-Sherbok, D. (2006). *The Paradox of Anti-Semitism*, p. 34. Retrieved from https://books.google.com/books

16.   *Synod of Laodicea (4th Century) – The Canons*. Retrieved from www.newadvent.org/fathers/3806.htm.

17.   *See*, Finto, Don (2001). *Your People Shall Be My People*. Bloomington, MN: Chosen Books.

18.   Strong's Exhaustive Concordance of the Bible. (n.d.) 4150 moed: appointed time, place, or meeting. In BibleHub.com. Retrieved May 13, 2024, from https://biblehub.com/hebrew/4150.htm.

19.   Vayikra/Leviticus 23:1 Stone Chumash

20.   Washington, George. "Washington versus Sunday Laws" and "Address to the Jews (by Washington)" *American State Papers Bearing on Sunday Legislation*. Ed. William Addison Blakely. Washington, D.C.: The Religious Liberty Association. 171-173. At archive.org/stream/ameri-canstatepapooblak#page/n6/mode/1up

21.   *Ibid*.

22.   Hakutizwi, Bruce. Why Chick-fil-a is America's Most Profitable Fast Food Franchise. Retrieved July 21, 2019 from https://us.businessesfor-sale.com/us/search/fast-food-franchises-for-sale/articles/why-chick-fil-a-is-americas-most-profitable-fast-food-franchise.

23.   Vayikra/Leviticus 23:7 Stone Chumash. Laborious work is work that one regards as a necessity: "essential work that will cause a significant loss if it is not performed."

24.   Francis, William (1997). *Celebrate the Feasts of the Lord*, p. 15. Alexandria, VA: Crest Books.

25. *Ibid.* p. 34-35.

26. *Ibid.* p. 44

27. Reshit Katshir, *Hebrew for Christians*. Retrieved from www.hebrew4christians.com/Holidays/Spring_Holidays/First_Fruits/first_fruits.html.

28. Francis, *Celebrate the Feasts*, p. 55.

29. *Ibid.*

30. *Ibid.* p. 67.

31. *Ibid.* p. 68.

32. Some scholars believe the scapegoat was simply released into the wilderness to wander and eventually die. Others insist that the individual leading the goat to the wilderness had to ensure that it died, so that it did not return to Jerusalem, or be encountered by anyone else, since it carried the collective national sin of Israel and was therefore defiled.

33. Francis, *Celebrate the Feasts*, p. 82.

34. Hunter, Ross and Mary, "The Year the Scarlet Thread Stopped Turning White – the importance of historical and cultural context," Esperanza Viva Bible Talk, January 28, 2017, http://evbibletalk.blogspot.com/2017/01/the-year-scarlet-thread-stopped-turning.html, quoting Rosh Hashanah 31b, Babylonian Talmud, Soncino Press Edition, retrieved on May 14, 2024.

35. *Ibid.* p. 91.

36. "Sukkot, the Feast of Tabernacles/Booths, celebrates the autumn harvest; a similarity to the Thanksgiving holiday observed in the United States which is not coincidental. Prior to making their way to the New World, the Pilgrims, themselves the victims of religious persecution, spent several years among Sephardic Jews in Holland. When they later celebrated the legendary first Thanksgiving, their conscious frame of reference was Sukkot." Retrieved from http://www.cyber-kitchen.com/rfcj/category.cgi?category=SUKKOT. *See also* MJAA (Oct. 1, 2012), *DID YOU KNOW: The Jewish Feast of Tabernacles Inspired America's Celebration of Thanksgiving?* http://www.mjaa.org/site/News2?page=NewsArticle&id=7861.

37. *See also,* Leviticus 23:41.

www.ingramcontent.com/pod-product-compliance
Lightning Source LLC
Chambersburg PA
CBHW070513160726
48003CB00004B/1544